TEACH YOURSELF TO PLAY

GUITAR
SONGS

ISBN 978-1-4950-4984-2

HAL•LEONARD®
CORPORATION
7777 W. BLUEMOUND RD. P.O. BOX 13819 MILWAUKEE, WI 53213

Visit Hal Leonard Online at
www.halleonard.com

CONTENTS

COME AS YOU ARE
Nirvana

Video Lesson – 12 minutes, 14 seconds

Tune Down 1 Whole Step: (low to high) D–G–C–F–A–D
Key of F♯ minor

Guitar Tone:

- Guitar Tone 1:
  - ❯ clean tone
  - ❯ flanger effect
  - ❯ light reverb
  - ❯ neck pickup
  - ❯ EQ: bass – 5, mid – 5, treble – 7

- Guitar Tone 2 (Chorus):
  - ❯ medium distortion
  - ❯ light reverb
  - ❯ bridge pickup
  - ❯ EQ: bass – 5, mid – 5, treble – 7

- Guitar Tone 3 (Guitar Solo):
  - ❯ heavy distortion
  - ❯ delay effect
  - ❯ EQ: bass – 5, mid – 5, treble – 7

Techniques:

- Open-Strum Transitions: many of the chord changes are preceded by strumming open notes. Use these as a way to make the chord change smoothly. The open strums give you a little extra time to get ready for the next chord.

- Vibrato: use a heavy dose of fret-hand vibrato during the Guitar Solo to get a singing quality out of the note. Keep the wrist loose and shake the note up and down.

Chords:
Pre-Chorus:

F♯sus4 A
1333 1   1 1 1

Chorus:

B5 D
1 3 3   1 3 2

Come as You Are

Words and Music by Kurt Cobain

Tune down one step:
(low to high) D-G-C-F-A-D

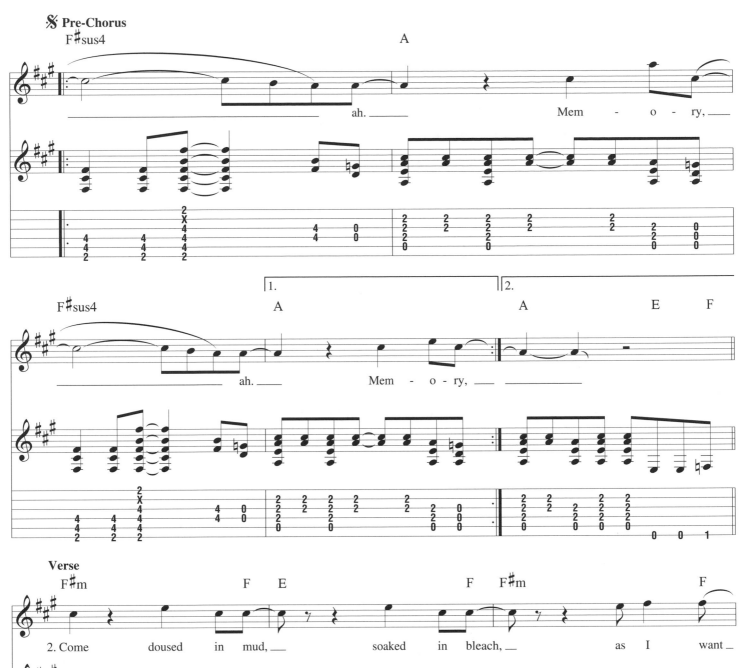

% Pre-Chorus

ah. _____ Mem - o - ry, _____

ah. _____ Mem - o - ry, _____

Verse

2. Come doused in mud, ___ soaked in bleach, ___ as I want ___

___ you ___ to be; _____ as a trend, ___ as a friend, ___

as an old _____ mem - o - ry, _____

Pre-Chorus

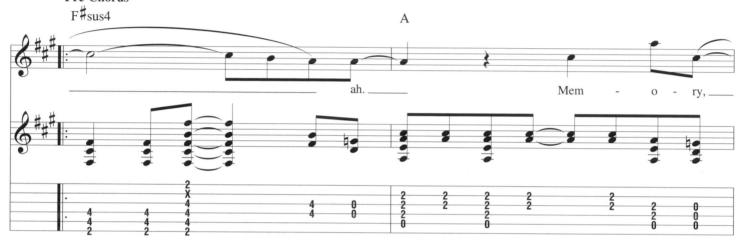

ah. _____ Mem - o - ry, _____

ah. _____ Mem - o - ry, _____

Chorus

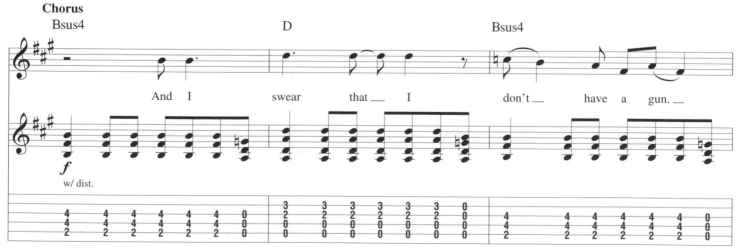

And I swear that ___ I don't ___ have a gun.

f
w/ dist.

No, I don't _____ have a gun. _____ No, I don't _____

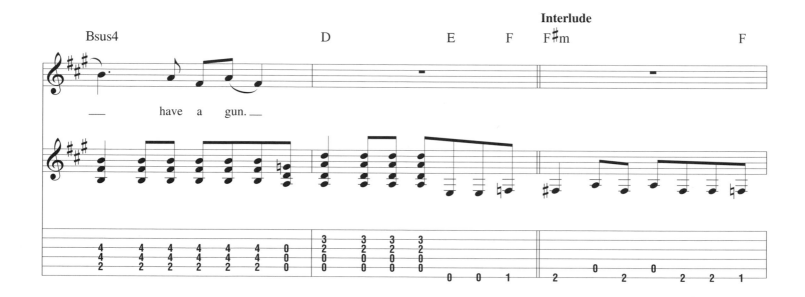

_____ have a gun. _____

Interlude

w/ heavy dist. & delay

Guitar Solo

Pre-Chorus

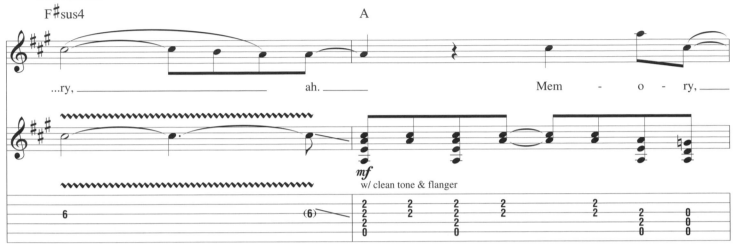

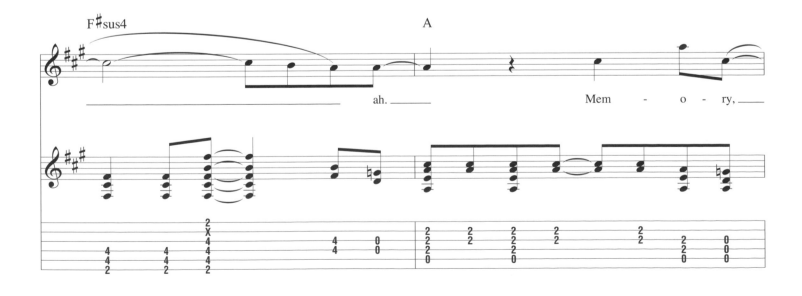

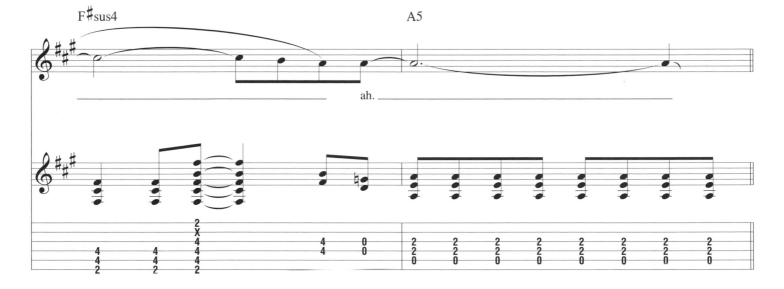

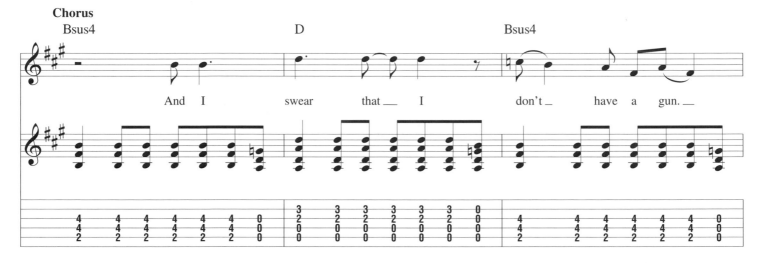

Chorus

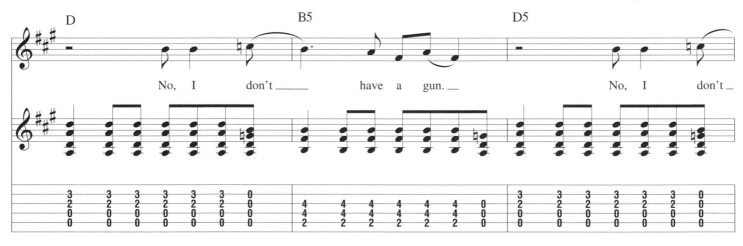

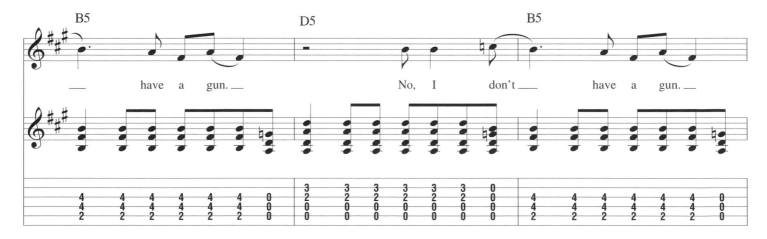

No, I don't ___ have a gun. ___

Outro

Mem - o - ry, _____ ah. ___

___ Mem - o - ry, ___

ah. ___

DO I WANNA KNOW?
Arctic Monkeys

Video Lesson – 12 minutes, 30 seconds

Standard Tuning: (low to high) E–A–D–G–B–E
Key of G minor

Guitar Tone:

- 12-string electric guitar

- light distortion

- light reverb

- tremolo effect

- neck pickup

- EQ: bass – 6, mid – 6, treble – 5

Techniques:

- 12-String Electric Guitar: the original song is played on a 12-string electric guitar, but don't fret if you don't have one. You can still play this on a regular 6-string and it will sound great. You could also use an octave pedal or add another guitar to play the riffs an octave up for a more authentic sound.

- Hammer-Ons: be aware of the two different types of hammer-ons in this song. Grace-note hammer-ons are played as quickly as possible with no time value, while the regular hammer-ons are played in a specific notated rhythm. Make sure each note "speaks" at equal volume.

- Slides: like the hammer-ons, there are both regular, rhythmic slides and grace-note slides (with no time value) in this song. Strive for clear rhythm and articulation—don't rush and keep the volume even throughout.

- Muting: Avoid letting the notes ring together. In the main riff, for example, notes on the 5th string and 4th string shouldn't ring together. Use one or both of your hands to stop notes from sounding together as you pick through each riff.

Do I Wanna Know?

Words by Alex Turner
Music by Arctic Monkeys

— 16 —

...that the nights __ were main - ly made __ for say - ing things __

__ both know...) __

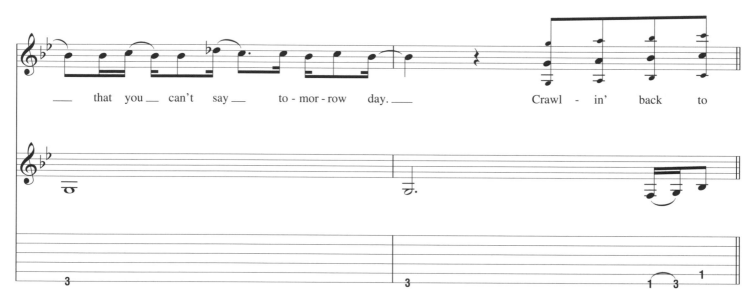

__ that you __ can't say __ to - mor - row day. __

Crawl - in' back to

Chorus

you. Ev - er thought of call - ing when __ you've had a few?

'Cause I al - ways

do. May-be I'm too bus-y be-ing yours to fall for some-

bod-y new. Now I've thought it through. Crawl-in' back to

Verse

you. 2. So have you ___ got the guts?

dim.

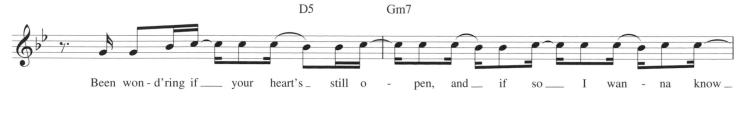

Gtr. tacet

D5   Gm7

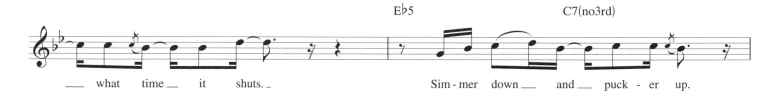

Been won - d'ring if ___ your heart's ___ still o - pen, and ___ if so ___ I wan - na know ___

Eb5   C7(no3rd)

___ what time ___ it shuts. ___   Sim - mer down ___ and ___ puck - er up.

D5   Gm7

I'm sor - ry to in - ter - rupt, ___ it's just, ___ I'm con - stant - ly on the cusp of ___

Eb5   C7(no3rd)

___ try   -   ing to kiss ___ you, ___   I don't know if ___

D5   Gm7

___ you ___   feel the same ___ as I ___ do. ___

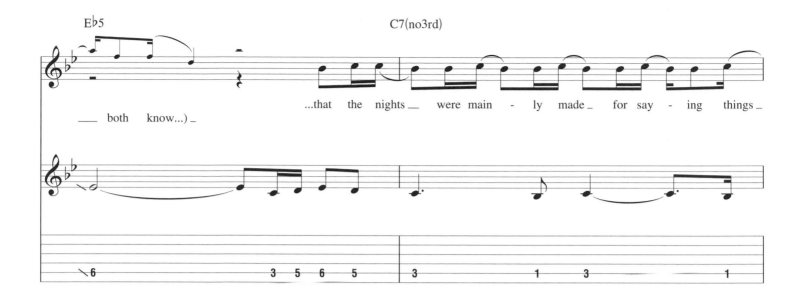

Eb5   C7(no3rd)

...that the nights ___ were main - ly made ___ for say - ing things ___
___ both know...) ___

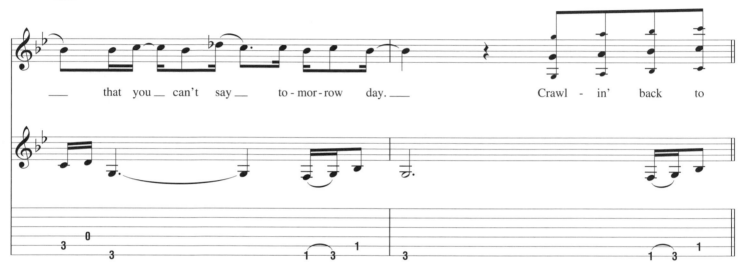

Gm7

___ that you ___ can't say ___ to - mor - row day. ___   Crawl - in' back to

Chorus

Gm7   Eb5   C7(no3rd)   D5

you.   Ev - er thought of call - ing when ___ you've had a few?   'Cause I al - ways

(Crawl - in' back to   you.   You've had a few. ___

Gm7

Was sort of hop - ing that __ you'd stay. _____ Ba - by, we __

___ you go. _____

E♭5   C7(no3rd)

...that the nights __ were main - ly made __ for say - ing things __

___ both know...) __

Gm7   E♭5

___ that you __ can't say __ to - mor - row day. __   Too bus - y be - ing

(Do I wan - na know? _____

yours to fall. _____   Ev - er thought of call - ing, dar - ling? _

(Sad to see ___ you go.) _____

—   Do you want me crawl - ing back ___ to you?

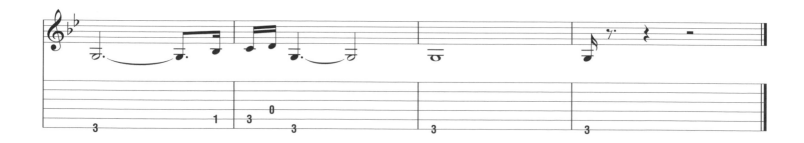

HEAVEN
Los Lonely Boys

Video Lesson – 24 minutes, 46 seconds

Tune Down 1/2 Step: (low to high) E♭–A♭–D♭–G♭–B♭–E♭
Key of G

Guitar Tone:

- Guitar Tone 1:
  - ❱ light distortion
  - ❱ light reverb
  - ❱ slapback delay
  - ❱ neck pickup
  - ❱ EQ: bass – 5, mid – 5, treble – 5

- Guitar Tone 2 (Verse):
  - ❱ clean tone
  - ❱ light reverb
  - ❱ neck pickup
  - ❱ EQ: bass – 5, mid – 5, treble – 5

Chords:
Verse:

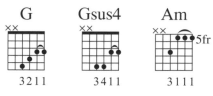

Bridge:

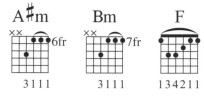

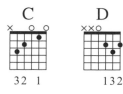

Scales:
Guitar Solos:

G Major Pentatonic Scale with Added 4th

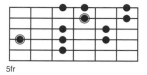

Techniques:

- Double-Stop Slides: when sliding both notes of a dyad, be sure to keep your fingers locked in the chord shape, maintaining the interval as you slide.

- Muted Notes: lightly touch the muted "X" notes with your fret hand, being careful not to fret the notes by pushing down too hard. Pick the muted notes normally, producing a "scratch" or "click" sound.

- Rake: to achieve a rake, drag your pick across the strings in a single motion while muting those strings with a fret-hand finger.

- String Bending: a variety of bends are employed in the Guitar Solos. Be sure to keep your bend pitches in tune! Practice these by fretting the target pitches first to hear how far you should bend the strings to nail the proper pitches. Make sure you use some support fingers behind the fretted note.

Heaven

Words and Music by Henry Garza, Joey Garza and Ringo Garza

Tune down 1/2 step:
(low to high) Eb-Ab-Db-Gb-Bb-Eb

Intro
Moderate Rock ♩ = 91

Va - ma - nos! _____

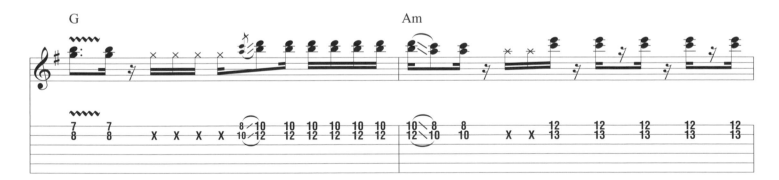

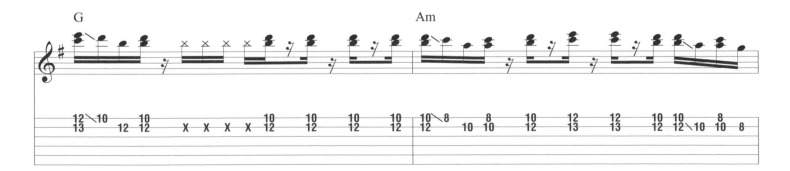

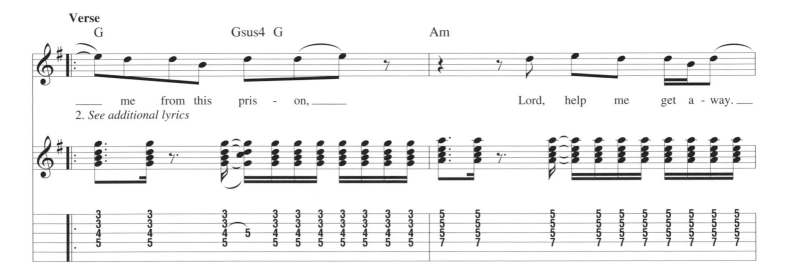

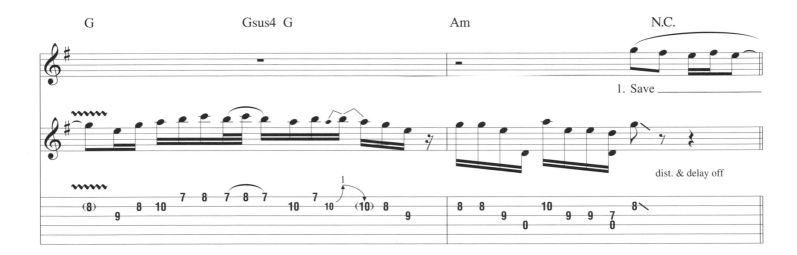

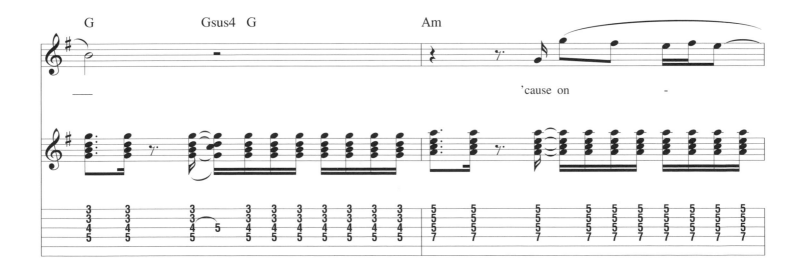

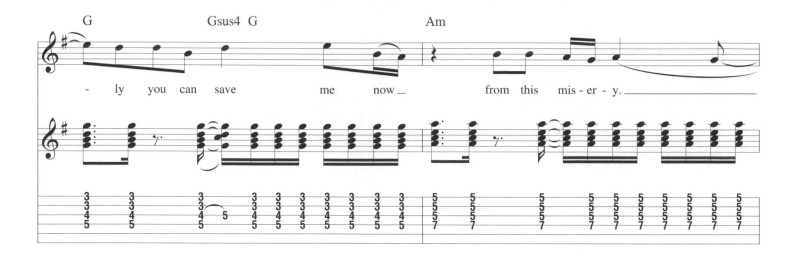

G   Gsus4   G   Am

-ly you can save   me now __   from this mis-er-y. __

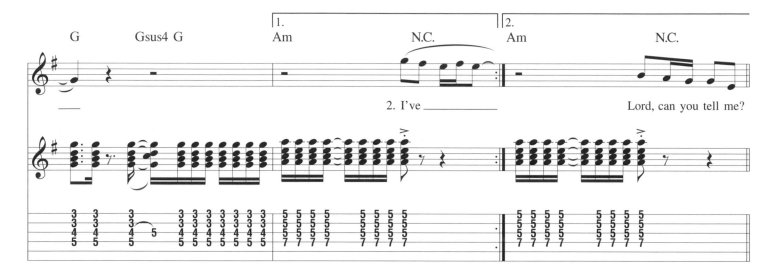

G   Gsus4 G   1. Am   N.C.   2. Am   N.C.

__   2. I've _____   Lord, can you tell me?

Interlude

G   Gsus4 G   Am   G   Gsus4 G

w/ dist. & slapback delay   *let ring –*

Verse

Am   N.C.   G   Gsus4 G   Am

3. I've _____ been locked up   way too long __   in this cra-zy world. __

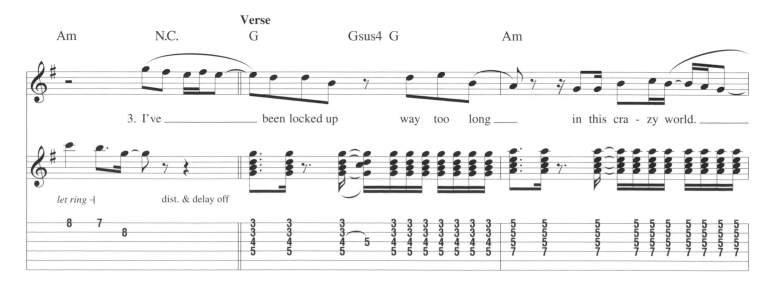

let ring ⊣   dist. & delay off

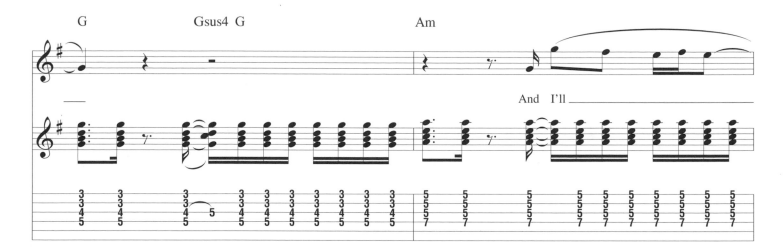

And I'll

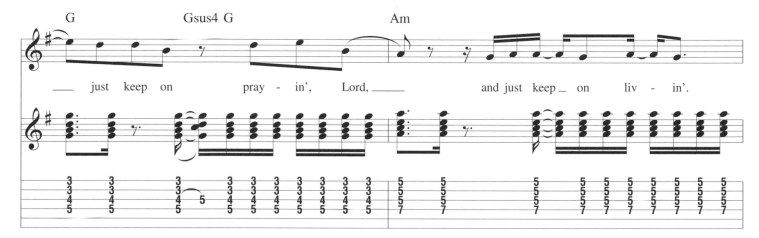

___ just keep on pray - in', Lord, _____ and just keep__ on liv - in'.

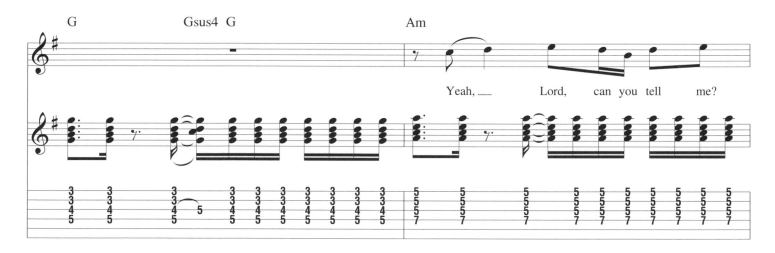

Yeah, ___ Lord, can you tell me?

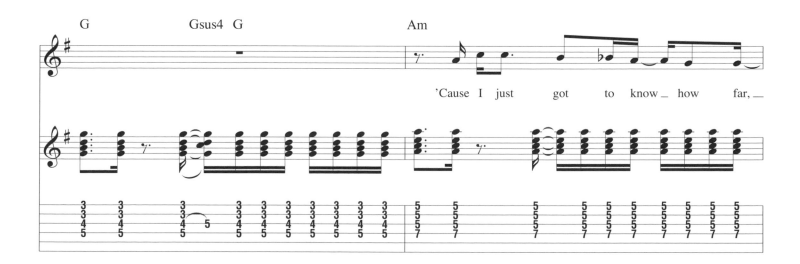

'Cause I just got to know__ how far, __

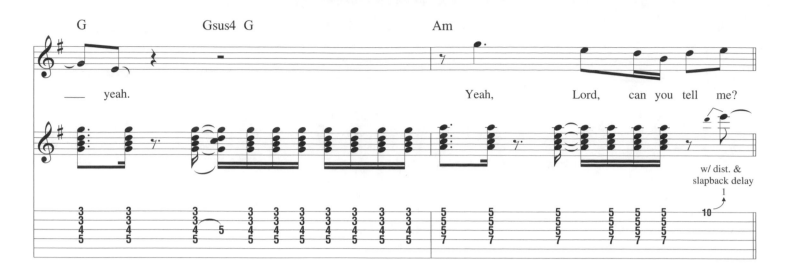

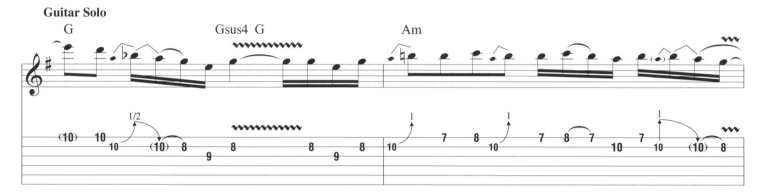

Guitar Solo

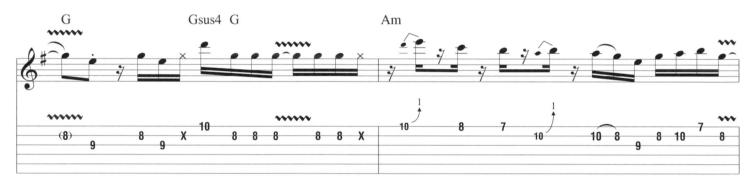

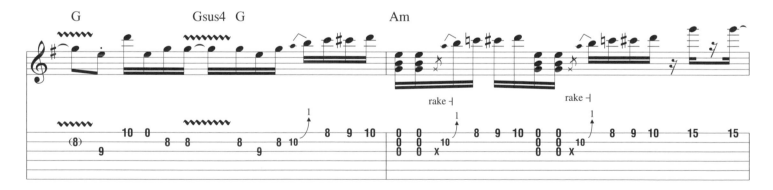

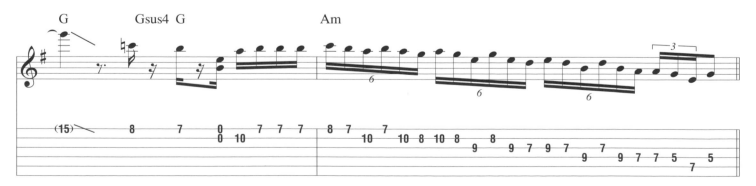

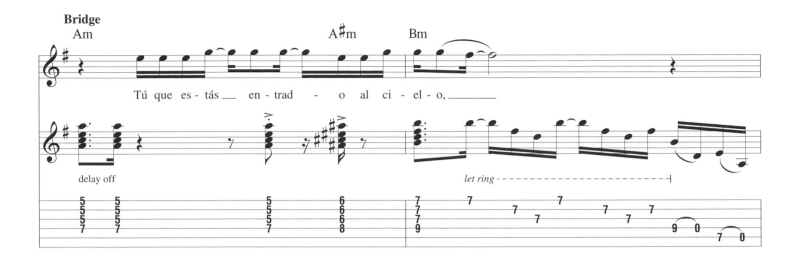

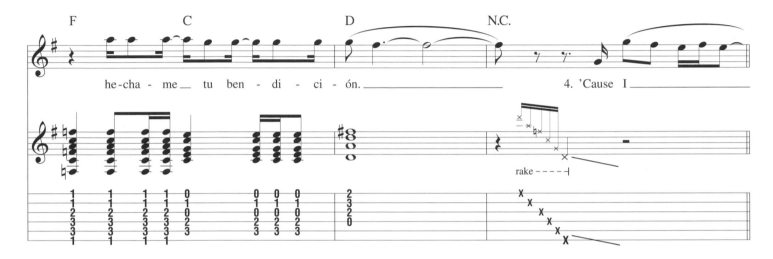

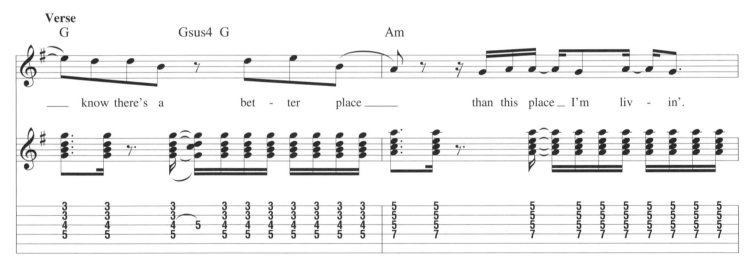

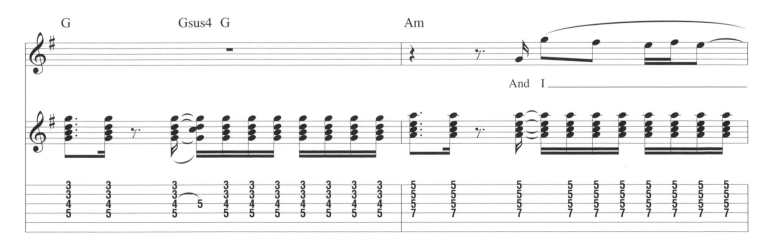

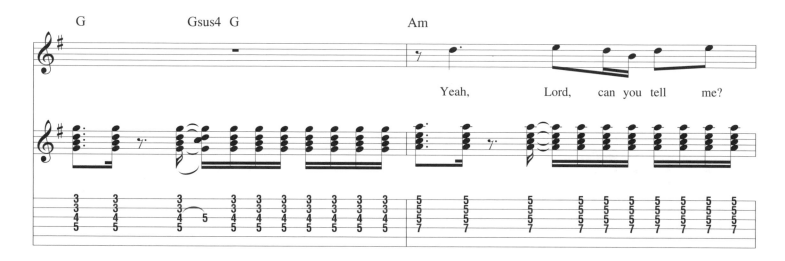

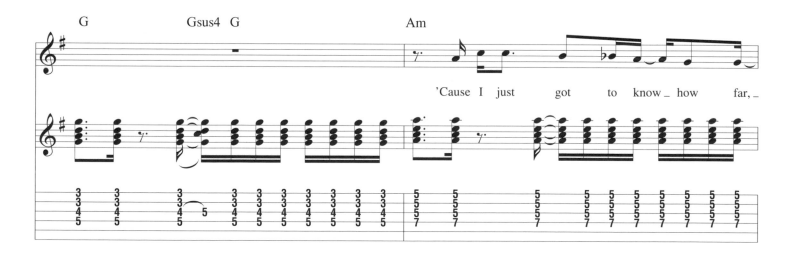

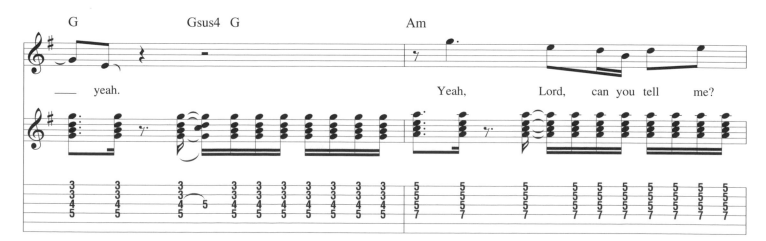

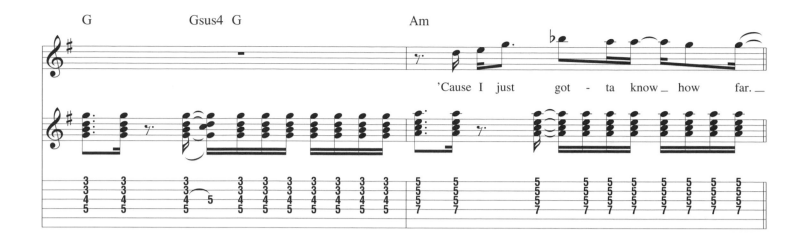

'Cause I just got - ta know how far.

Outro-Guitar Solo

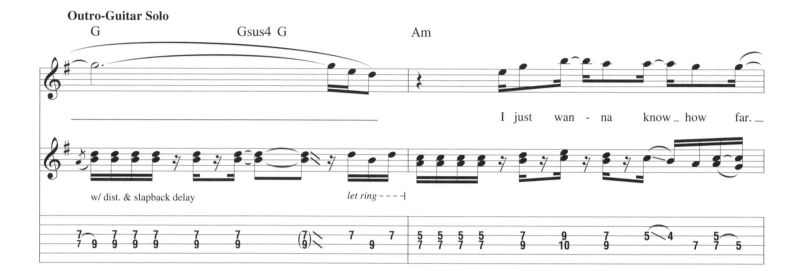

I just wan - na know how far.

w/ dist. & slapback delay

let ring - - - -

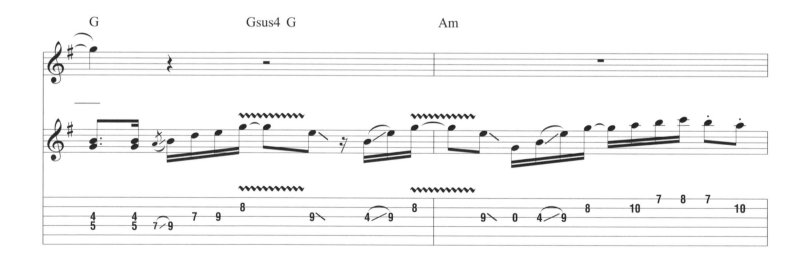

let ring - - - - -

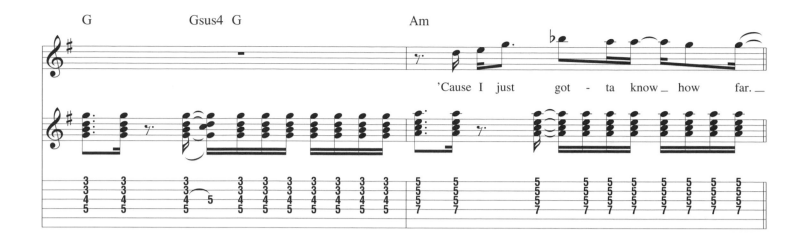

'Cause I just got - ta know how far.

Outro-Guitar Solo

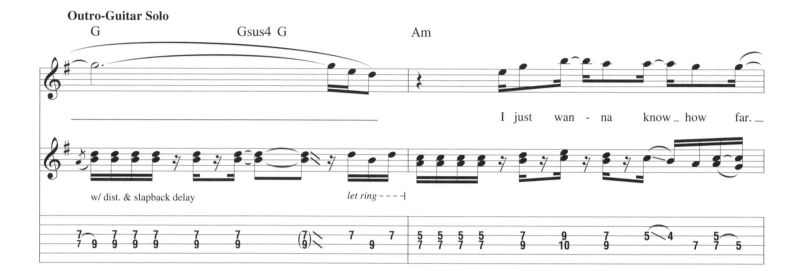

I just wan - na know how far.

w/ dist. & slapback delay

let ring - - - -

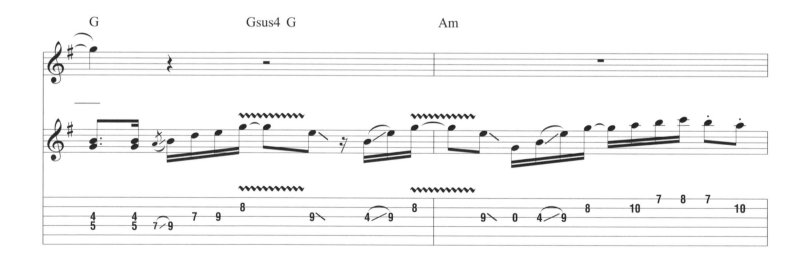

let ring - - - - -

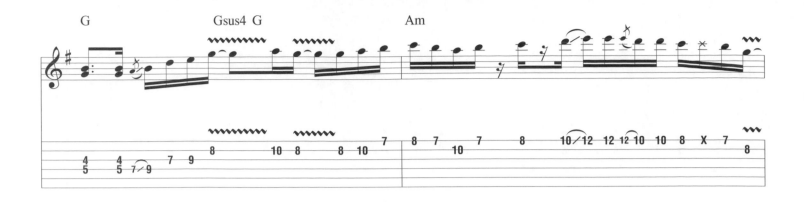

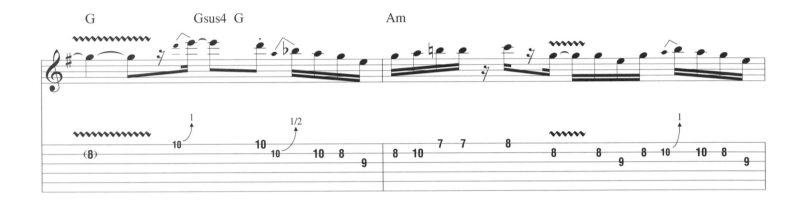

Fade out

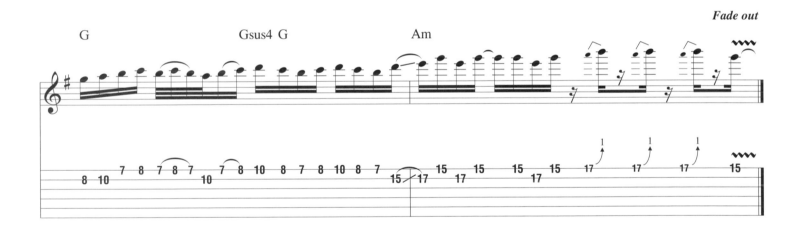

Additional Lyrics

2. I've been lost in my own place
   And I'm gettin' weary.
   And I know that I need to change
   My ways of livin'.
   Lord, can you tell me?

HERE WITHOUT YOU
3 Doors Down

Video Lesson – 15 minutes, 54 seconds

Tune Down 1/2 Step: (low to high) E♭–A♭–D♭–G♭–B♭–E♭
Key of B minor

Guitar Tone:

- electric guitar (or acoustic guitar)

- light reverb

- chorus

- EQ: bass – 5, mid – 6, treble – 6

Chords:

Bridge:

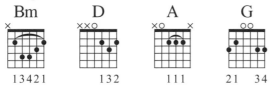

Bm   D   A   G

13421   132   111   21   34

Arpeggios:

Intro/Verse:

Bm Arpeggio   G Arpeggio

A Arpeggio

Chorus:

D Arpeggio   A Arpeggio

Bm(add4) Arpeggio

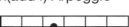

Techniques:

- Barre Chords: keep your 1st finger straight and flat and make sure all fretted notes ring clearly. You might find it helpful to roll your 1st finger a bit to the outside (towards the thumb) to help it remain flat.

- Arpeggios: most chords in this song are played as arpeggios. Make sure all notes are ringing clearly. For picking accuracy, you may find it helpful to anchor your pick hand by lightly resting your pinky on the pickguard.

Here Without You

Words and Music by Matt Roberts, Brad Arnold, Christopher Henderson and Robert Harrell

Tune down 1/2 step:
(low to high) E♭-A♭-D♭-G♭-B♭-E♭

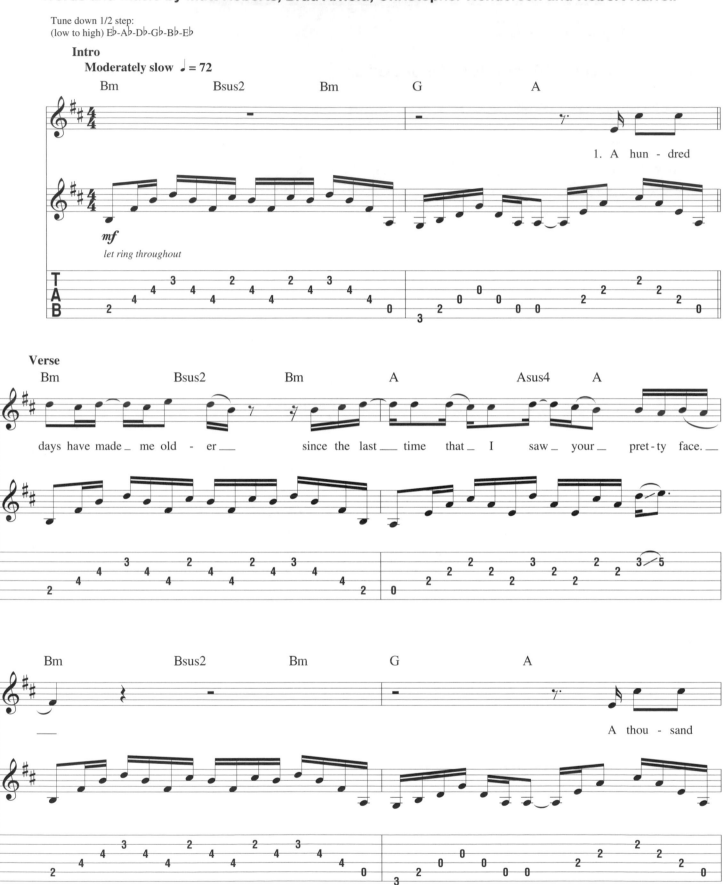

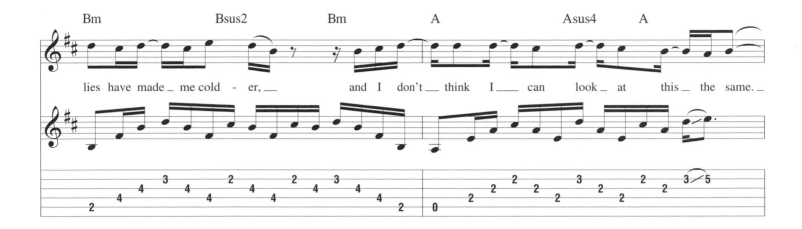

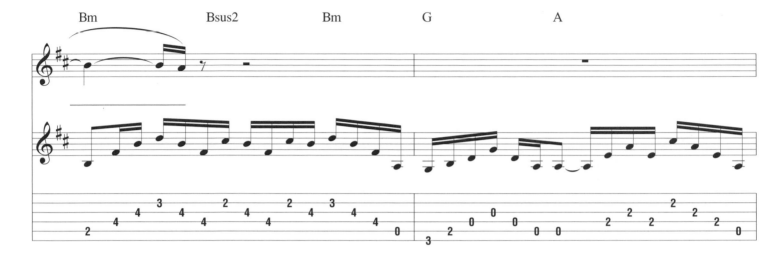

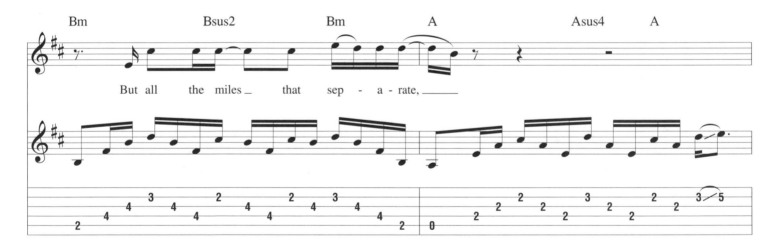

Chorus

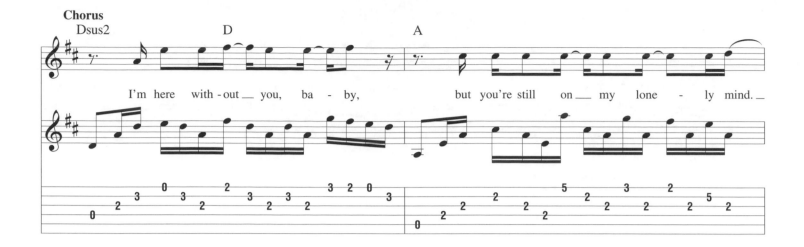

I'm here with-out ___ you, ba - by, but you're still on ___ my lone - ly mind. ___

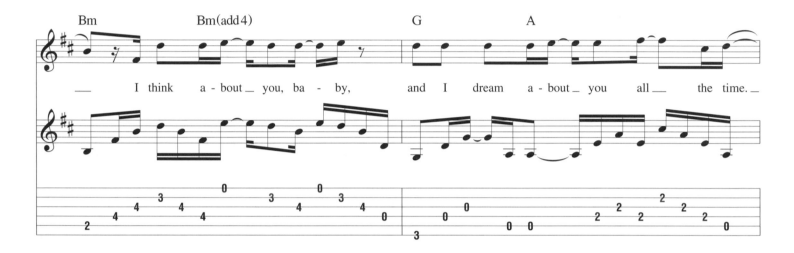

___ I think a - bout ___ you, ba - by, and I dream a - bout ___ you all ___ the time. ___

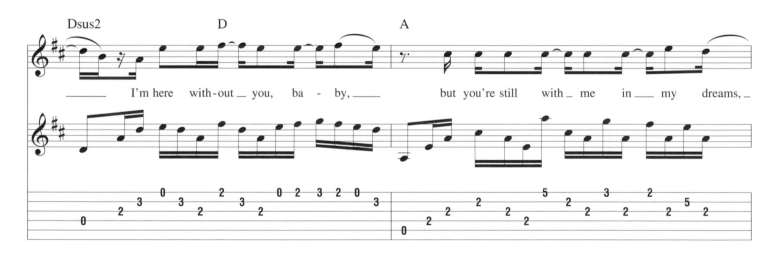

___ I'm here with-out ___ you, ba - by, ___ but you're still with ___ me in ___ my dreams, ___

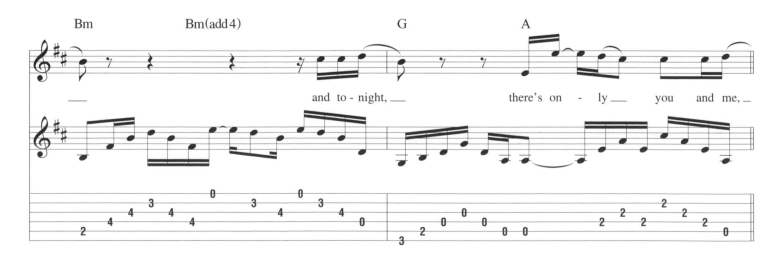

___ and to - night, ___ there's on - ly ___ you and me, ___

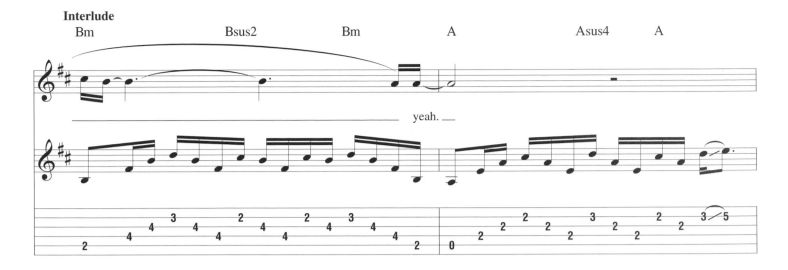

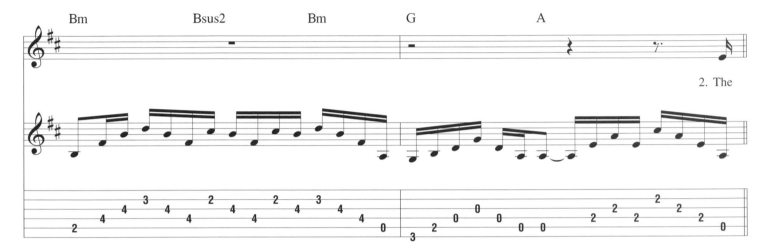

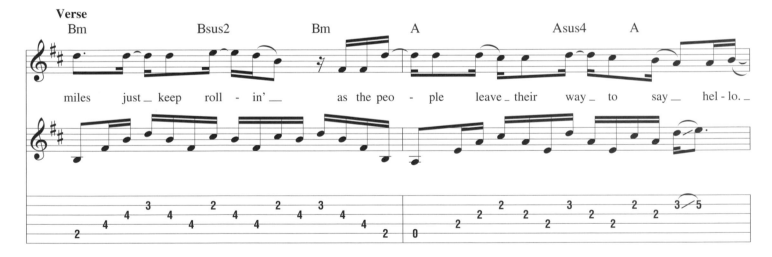

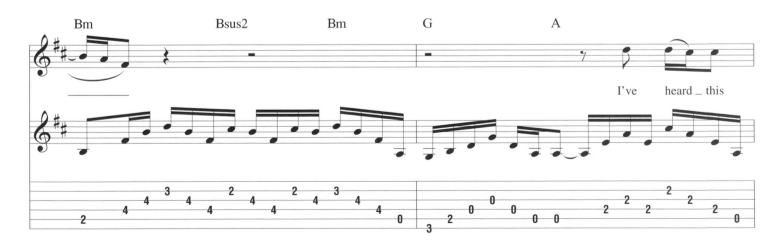

life _ is o - ver-rat - ed, _ but I hope _ that it _ gets bet - ter _ as _ we go. _

_ Oh, _____ yeah, _____ yeah.

Chorus

I'm here with-out _ you, ba - by, but you're still on _ my lone - ly mind. _

_ I think a-bout _ you, ba - by, and I dream a-bout _ you all _____ the time. _

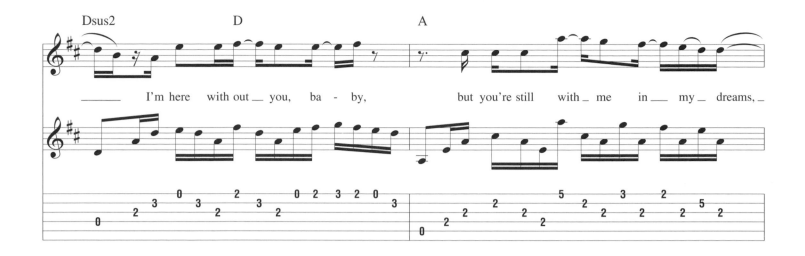

I'm here with out __ you, ba - by, but you're still with __ me in __ my __ dreams, __

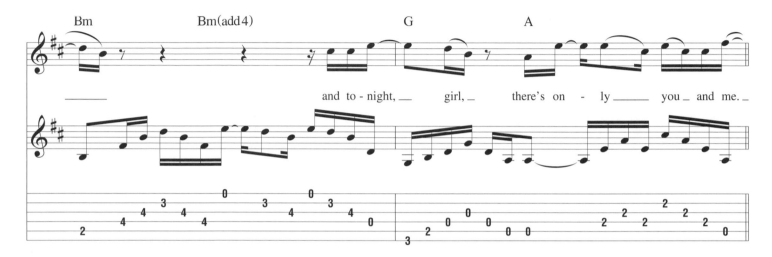

__ and to - night, __ girl, __ there's on - ly _____ you __ and me. __

Bridge

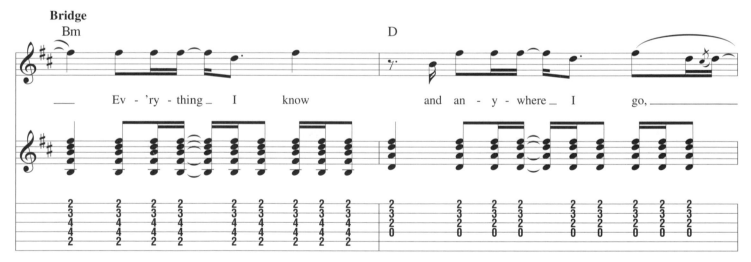

__ Ev - 'ry - thing __ I know and an - y - where __ I go, _____

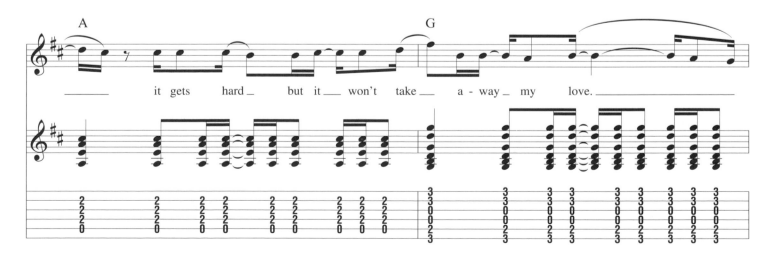

_____ it gets hard __ but it __ won't take __ a - way __ my love. _____

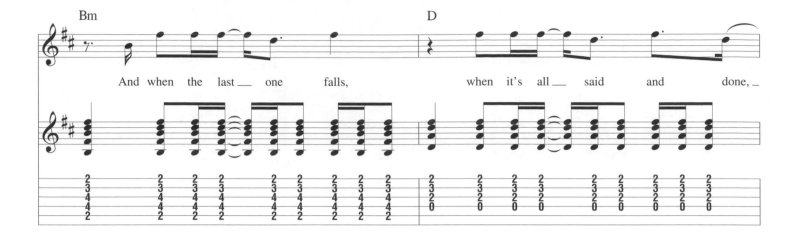

And when the last ___ one falls, when it's all ___ said and done, ___

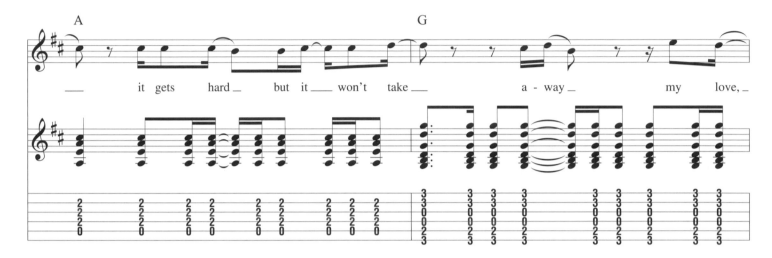

___ it gets hard ___ but it ___ won't take ___ a - way ___ my love, ___

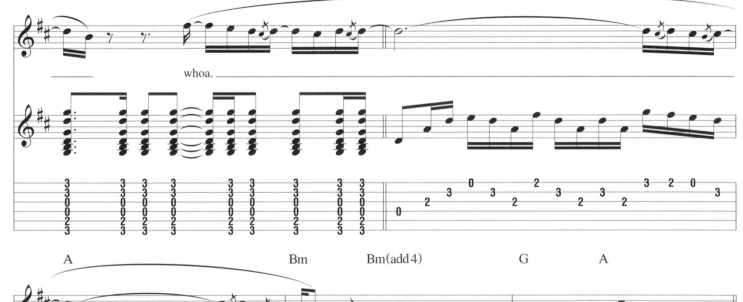

Interlude

___ whoa. ___

Chorus

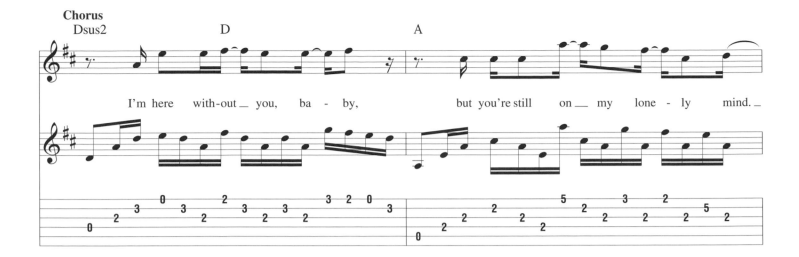

I'm here with-out __ you, ba - by, but you're still on __ my lone - ly mind. __

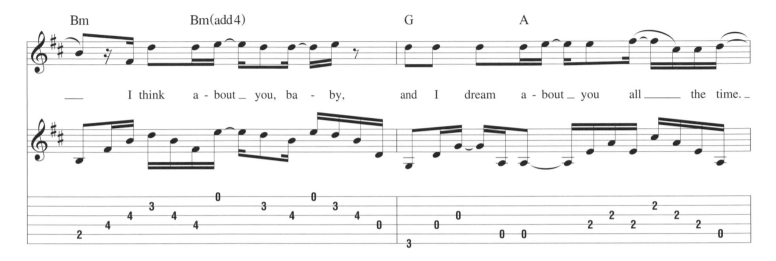

__ I think a - bout __ you, ba - by, and I dream a - bout __ you all _____ the time. __

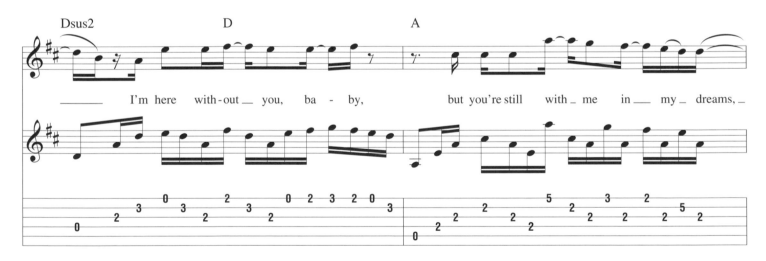

_____ I'm here with-out __ you, ba - by, but you're still with __ me in __ my __ dreams, __

_____ and to - night, __ girl, __ there's on - ly _____ you __ and me, __

Outro

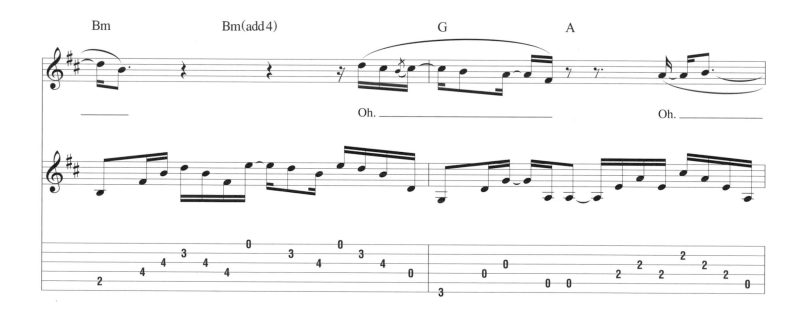

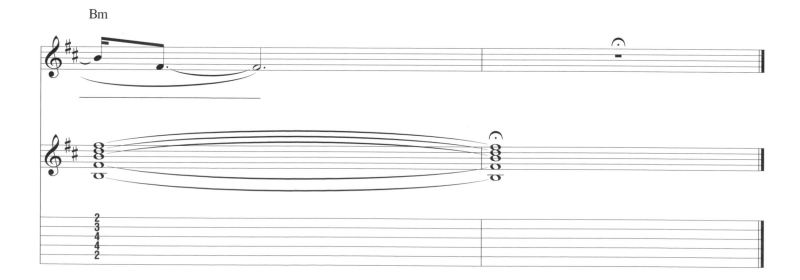

LEARN TO FLY
Foo Fighters

Video Lesson – 14 minutes, 40 seconds

Standard Tuning: (low to high) E–A–D–G–B–E
Key of B

Guitar Tone:

- medium distortion
- light reverb
- bridge pickup
- EQ: bass – 6, mid – 5, treble – 6

Chords:

Verse:

Bsus2 F#m11 E5

13411   T 31   114

Chorus:

Bsus4   G   Asus4   A

134   21 34   113   111

Bridge:

D   E   D/F#

132   231   1 23

Techniques:

- Octaves: fret these intervals with the 1st and 3rd fingers. Flatten the 1st finger slightly so it mutes the string in between the octaves. Strum through the octave notes.

- Thumb-Fretting: for the F#m11 chord, wrap your fret-hand thumb over the neck to fret the 6th string, 2nd fret. If you're not comfortable using your thumb, you can use your 1st finger instead, but it makes the chord more difficult to fret.

- Strumming: use downstrokes and upstrokes to strum the Chorus chords. Catch the lower strings with a downstroke and the higher strings with an upstroke.

Learn to Fly

Words and Music by Taylor Hawkins, Nate Mendel and Dave Grohl

Intro

Moderately fast Rock ♩ = 136

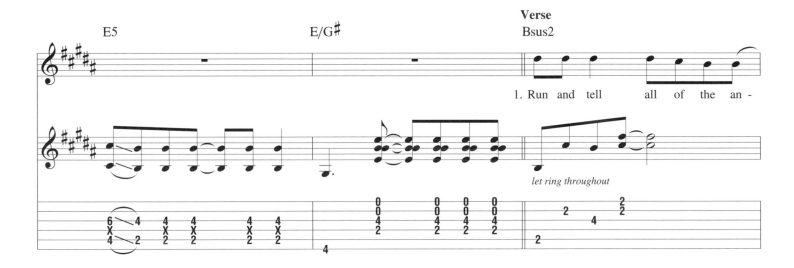

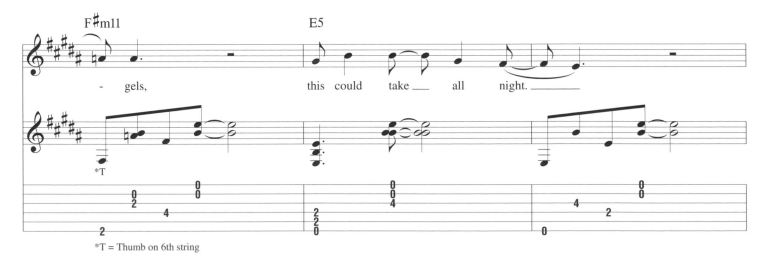

*T = Thumb on 6th string

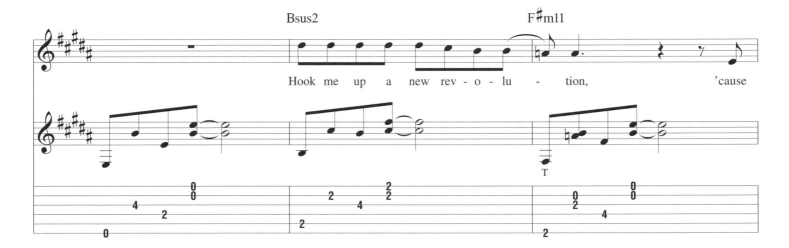

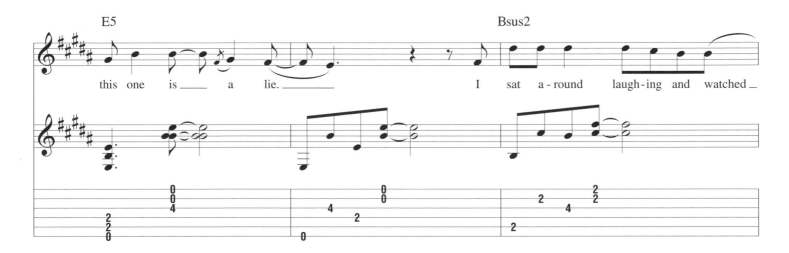

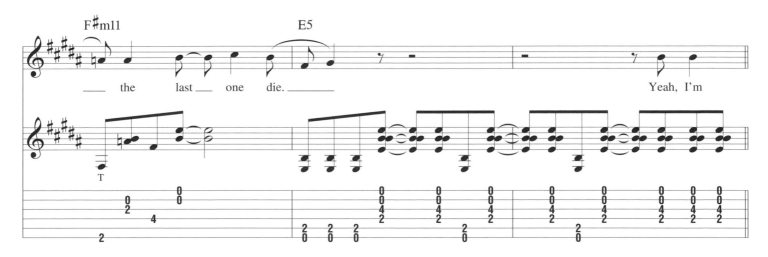

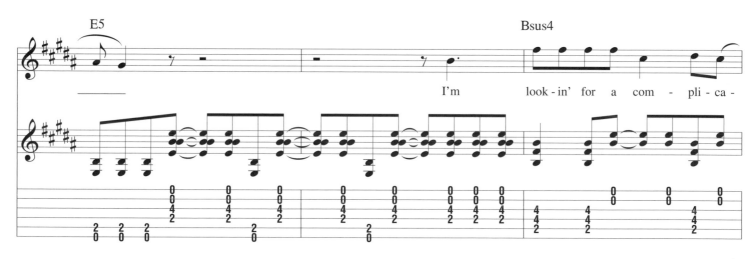

To Coda 1 ⊕

To Coda 2 ⊕

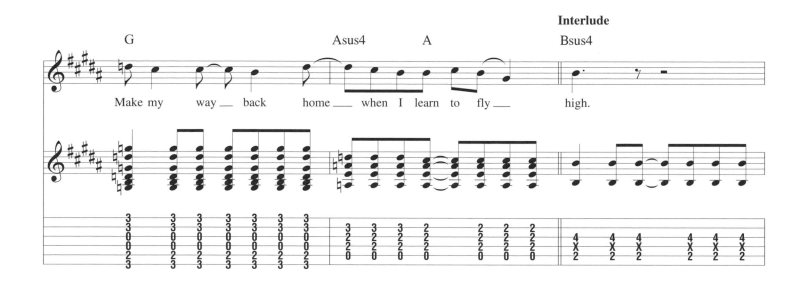

Make my way — back home — when I learn to fly — high.

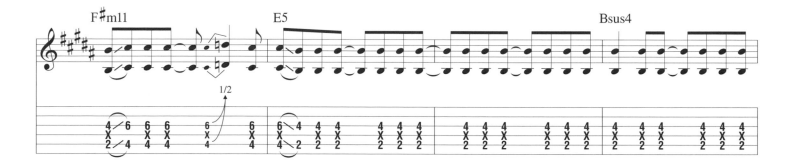

2. I

Verse

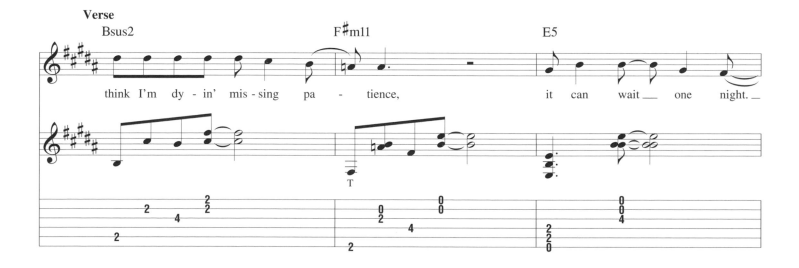

think I'm dy - in' mis - sing pa - tience, it can wait — one night.

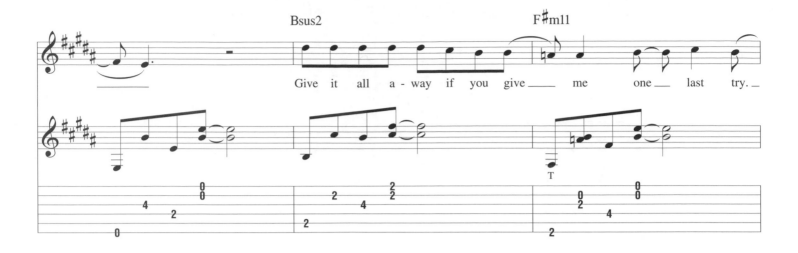

Bsus2   F#m11

Give it all a - way if you give ____ me one __ last try. __

E5   Bsus2   F#m11

We'll live hap - pi - ly ev - er trapped _ if you _

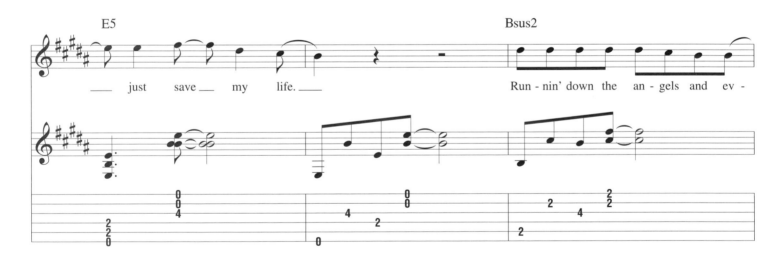

E5   Bsus2

_ just save _ my life. __ Run - nin' down the an - gels and ev -

D.S. al Coda 1

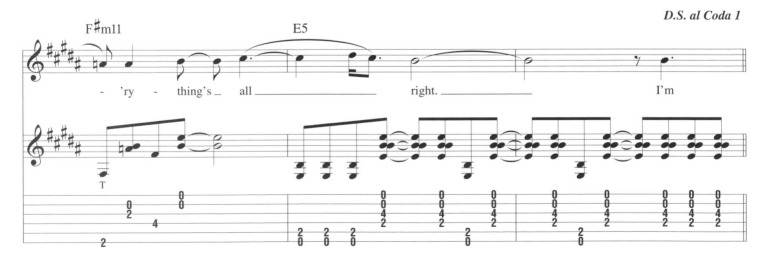

F#m11   E5

- 'ry - thing's _ all _____ right. _____ I'm

⊕ Coda 1

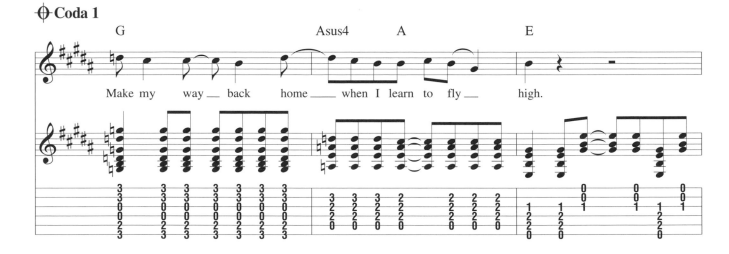

Make my way back home when I learn to fly high.

Make my way back home when I learn to...

Bridge

Fly a - long

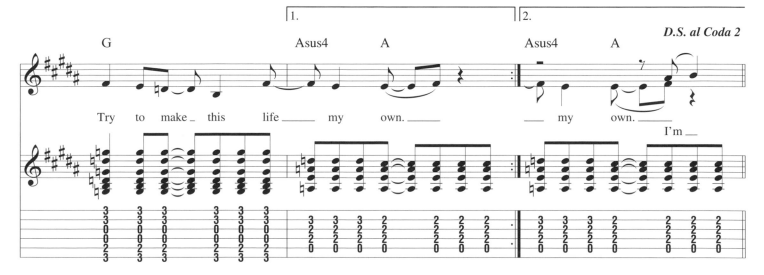

with me, I can't quite make it a - lone.

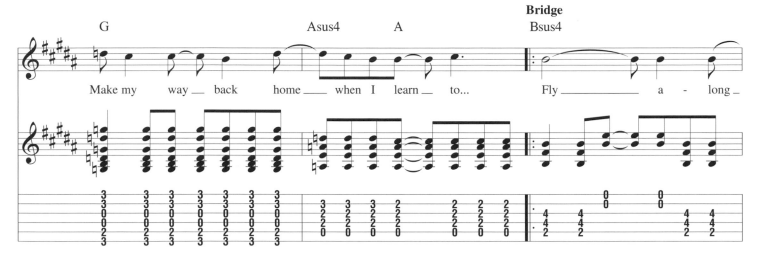

1.

Try to make this life my own.

2.

D.S. al Coda 2

my own. I'm

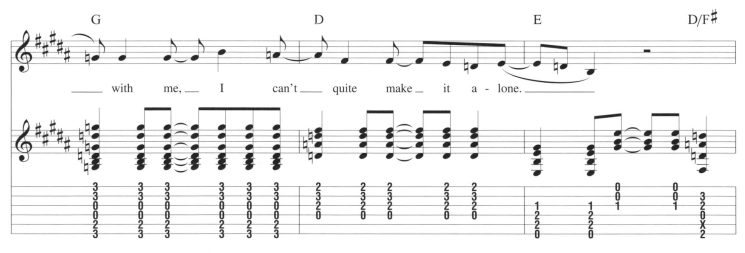

— 51 —

⊕ Coda 2

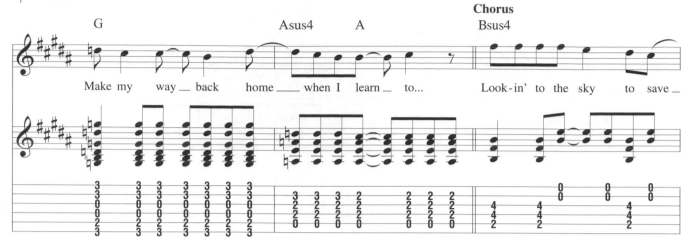

Make my way ___ back home ___ when I learn ___ to... Look-in' to the sky to save ___

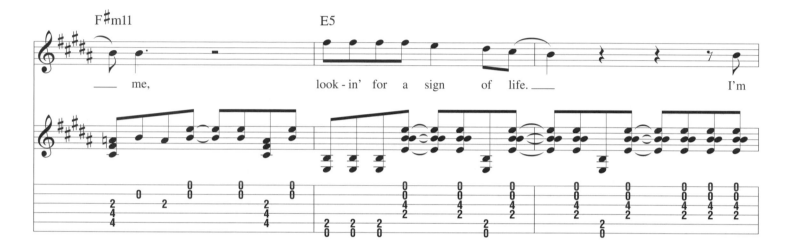

___ me, look - in' for a sign of life. ___ I'm

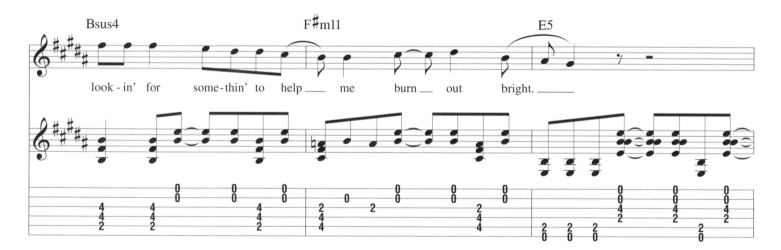

look - in' for some-thin' to help ___ me burn ___ out bright. ___

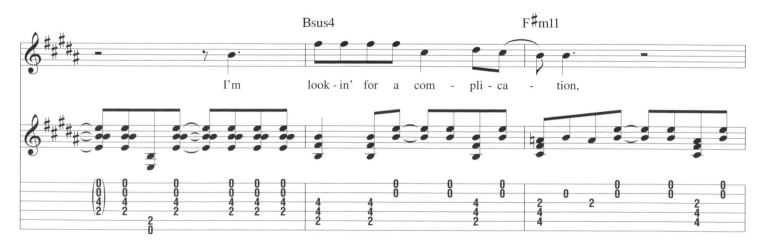

I'm look - in' for a com - pli - ca - tion,

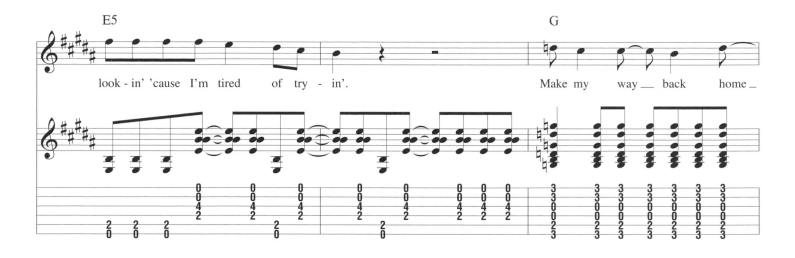

look - in' 'cause I'm tired of try - in'. Make my way __ back home __

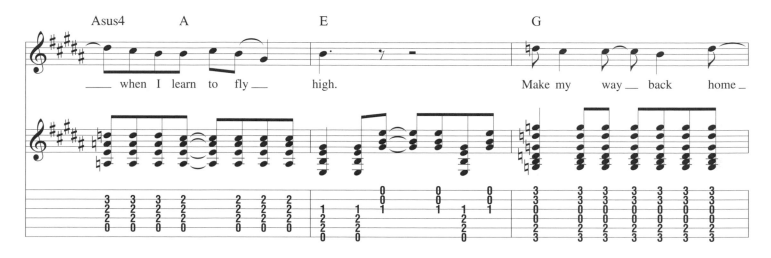

__ when I learn to fly __ high. Make my way __ back home __

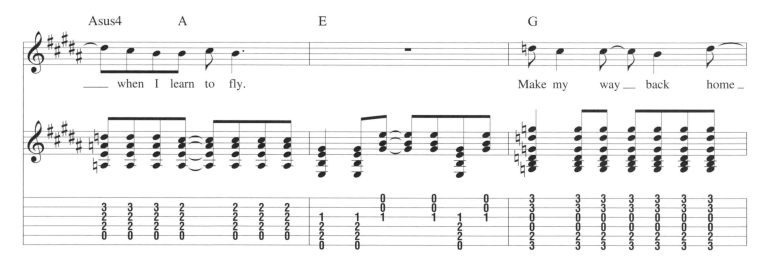

__ when I learn to fly. Make my way __ back home __

Outro

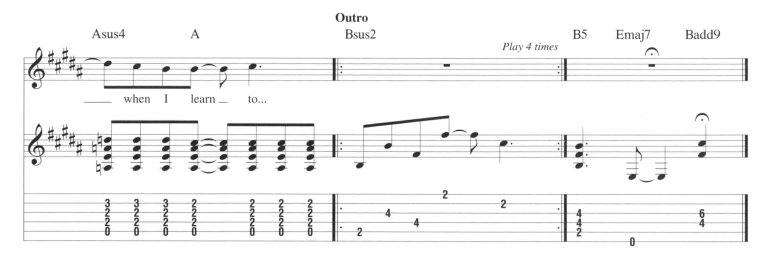

__ when I learn __ to...

PLUSH
Stone Temple Pilots

Video Lesson – 15 minutes, 6 seconds

Standard Tuning: (low to high) E–A–D–G–B–E
Key of G

Guitar Tone:

- heavy distortion
- chorus effect
- bridge pickup
- EQ: bass – 6, mid – 6, treble – 7

Chords:
Intro:

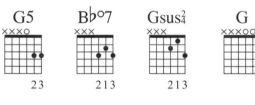

G5   Bb°7   Gsus$^2_4$ G

Verse:

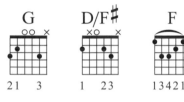

G   D/F#   F

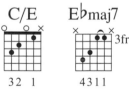

C/E   Ebmaj7

Chorus:

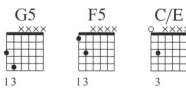

G5   F5   C/E

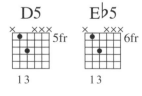

D5   Eb5

Arpeggios:
Bridge:

D Arpeggio

Csus2 Arpeggio

G/B Arpeggio

Techniques:

- Muted Strums: keep your fret hand lightly in contact with the strings, being careful not to accidentally fret any notes by pressing down too hard. Strum the muted strings, producing a "click" type sound. You can also assist the damping by using your pick hand to palm mute the strings near the bridge.

- Open-Strum Transitions: notice the open strummed notes during the Bridge at the end of each measure (while you hold down the D note on the 2nd string, 3rd fret). Use this for smoother chord changes. As you strum the open notes, prepare your fingers for the next chord.

Plush

Words and Music by Scott Weiland, Dean DeLeo, Robert DeLeo and Eric Kretz

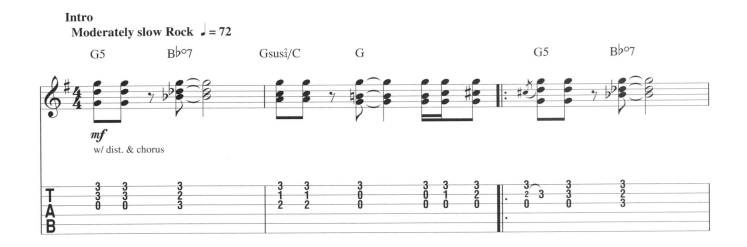

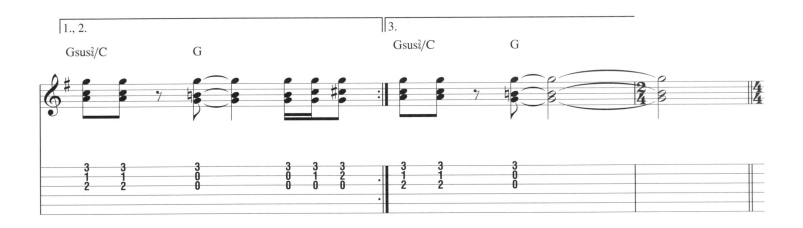

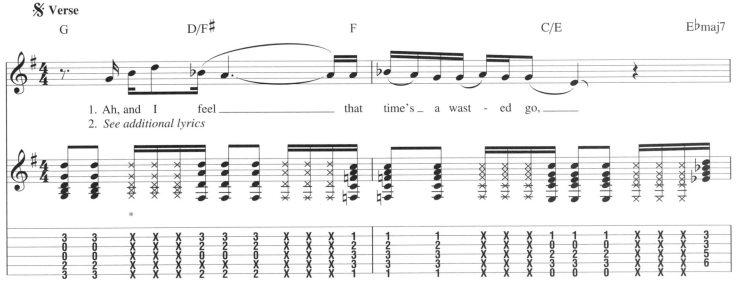

*Muted strings produce occasional random harmonics throughout.

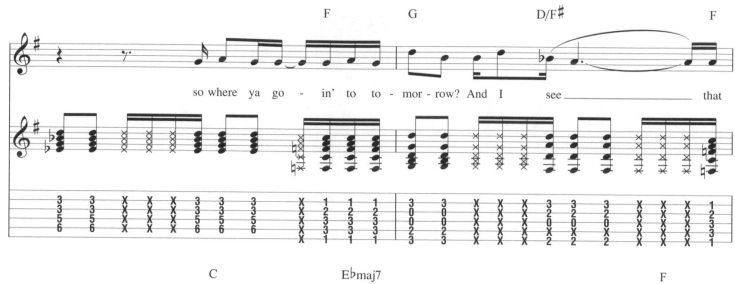

so where ya go - in' to to - mor - row? And I   see _____ that

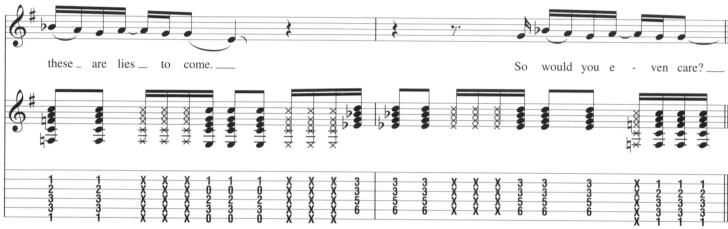

these _ are lies _ to come. ___   So   would you e - ven care? ___

Bridge

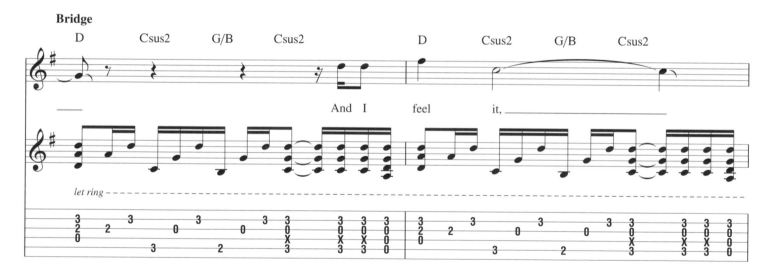

___   And I   feel   it, _____

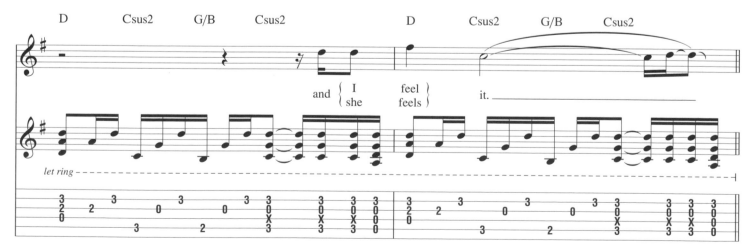

and { I / she } { feel / feels } it. _____

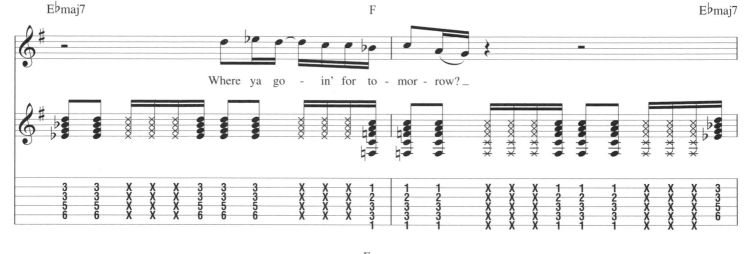

Where ya go - in' for to - mor - row? _

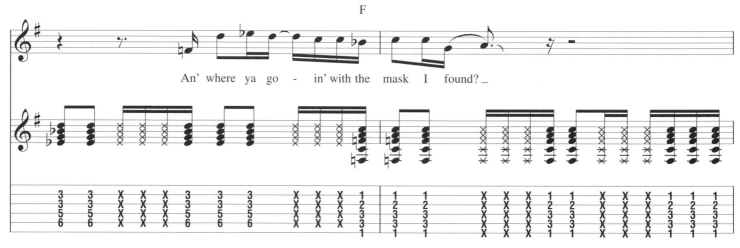

An' where ya go - in' with the mask I found? _

And I feel, _ and I feel _____ when the dogs be - gin _ to smell _ her.

To Coda 1

To Coda 2

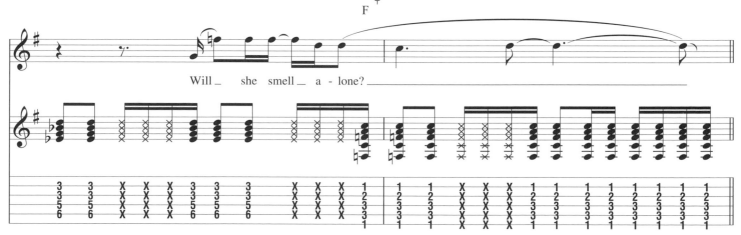

Will _ she smell _ a - lone? _____

Interlude

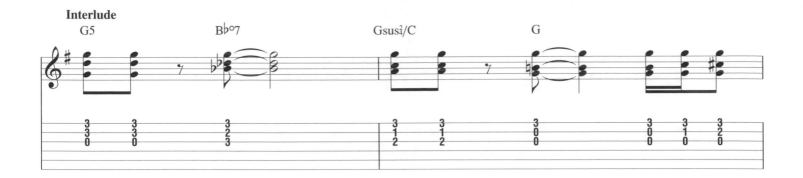

D.S. al Coda 1

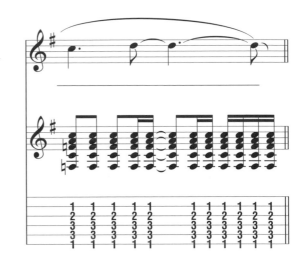

Coda 1

Chorus

When ___ the dogs ___ do find ___ her, ___ we got time, ___ time ___ (to) wait ___ for to-

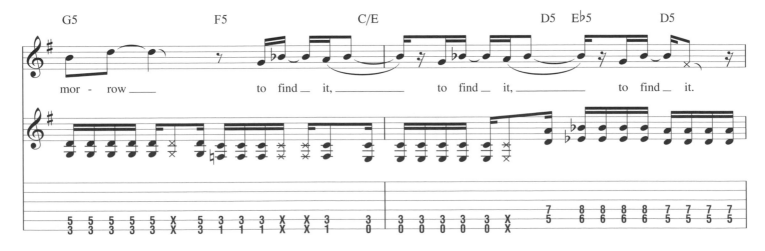

mor - row _____ to find ___ it, _____ to find ___ it, _____ to find ___ it.

When ___ the dogs _ do find _ her, ___ we got time _ time ___ (to) wait _ for to-

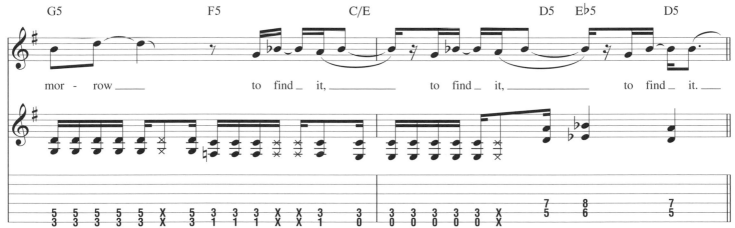

mor - row _____ to find _ it, _____ to find _ it, _____ to find _ it. ___

Interlude

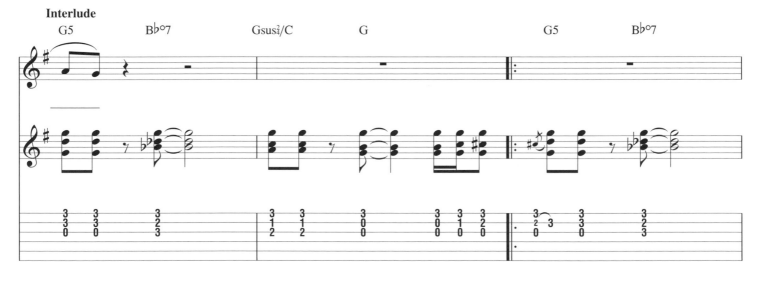

|1., 2. | |3. | *D.S.S. al Coda 2* | ⊕ **Coda 2**

Chorus

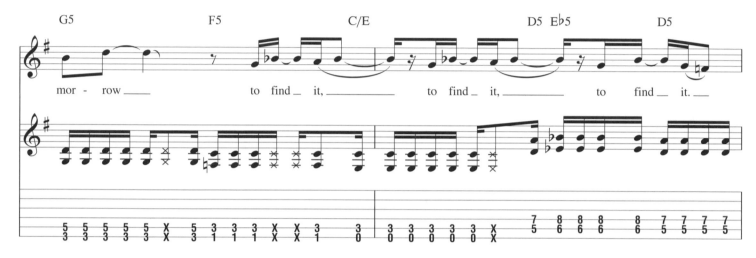

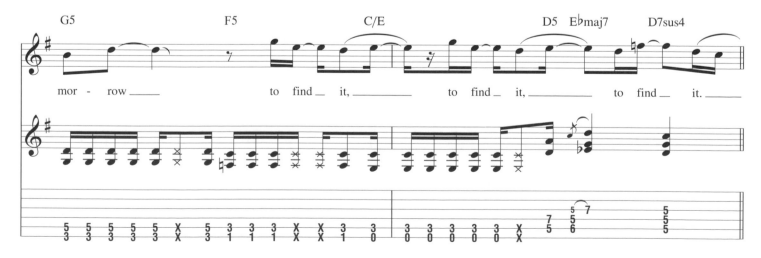

Outro

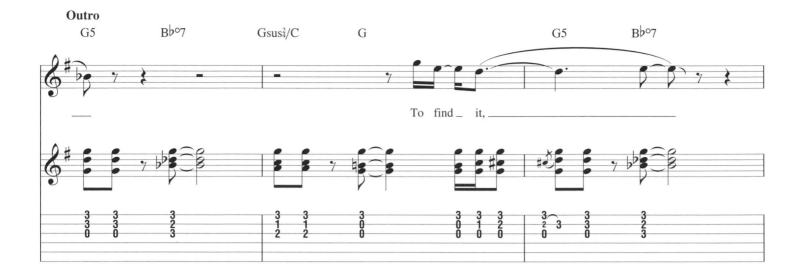

To find it,

to find it,

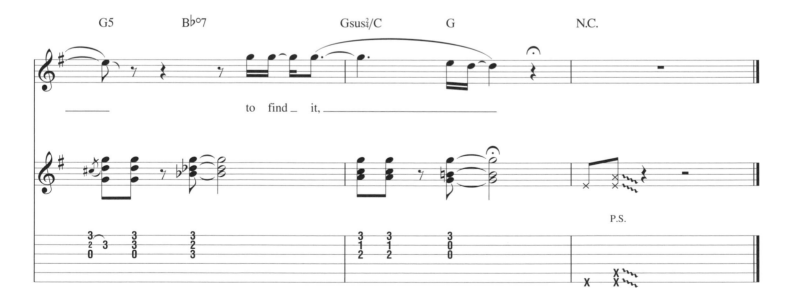

to find it,

Additional Lyrics

2. Ah, and I feel so much depends on the weather,
   So is it raining in your bedroom?
   And I see that these are the eyes of disarray.
   So would you even care?

SANTERIA
Sublime

Video Lesson – 16 minutes, 20 seconds

Standard Tuning: (low to high) E–A–D–G–B–E
Key of E

Guitar Tone:

- clean tone
- light reverb
- bridge pickup
- EQ: bass – 6, mid – 5, treble – 7

Chords:

Intro:

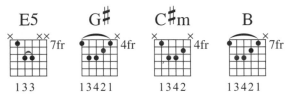

Verse:

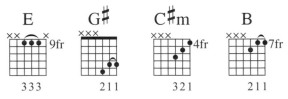

Chorus:

A   D#m

211   1342

Scales:

Guitar Solo:

E Major Pentatonic Scale

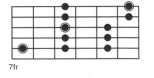

Techniques:

- Rests: be mindful of the rests during the Verse. Mute the notes by either damping with the pick hand, lifting off with the fret hand, or a combination of both.

- Arpeggios: look for the big picture in the Chorus. You'll want to hold down full chords. Notice when the chords change. Don't look at the parts as individual notes; you'll hold chords down for the entire Chorus.

- String Bending: a variety of bends are employed in the Guitar Solo. Be sure to keep your bend pitches in tune! Practice these by fretting the target pitches first to hear how far you should bend the strings to nail the proper pitches. Make sure you use some support fingers behind the fretted note.

- Hammer-Ons: be careful not to rush the hammer-ons in the Guitar Solo. The notes should fall in an even rhythm.

- Double-Stop Bends: use either your 3rd finger barred, or 3rd and 4th fingers to fret the double-stop bends in the Guitar Solo.

Santeria

Words and Music by Brad Nowell, Eric Wilson and Floyd Gaugh

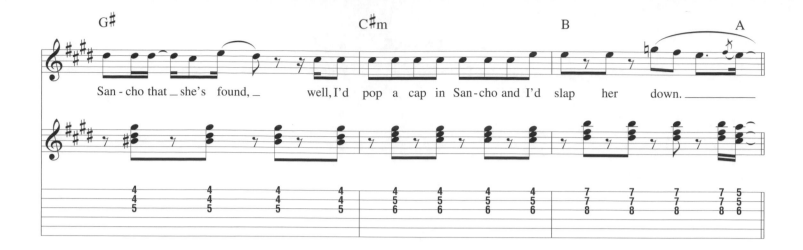

Sancho that she's found, well, I'd pop a cap in Sancho and I'd slap her down.

Chorus

What I really wanna know, my baby, mm. What I really wanna say

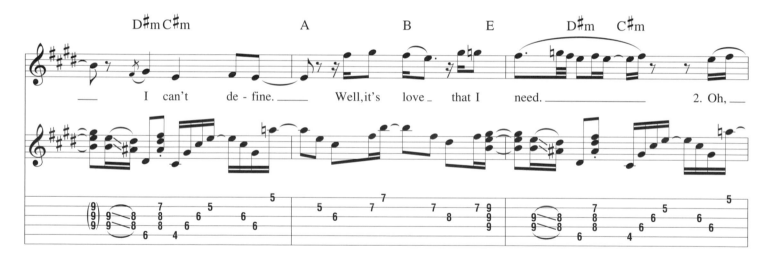

I can't define. Well, it's love that I need. 2. Oh,

% Verse

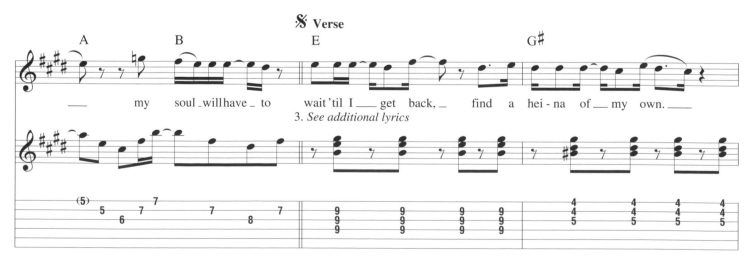

my soul will have to wait 'til I get back, find a heina of my own.
3. *See additional lyrics*

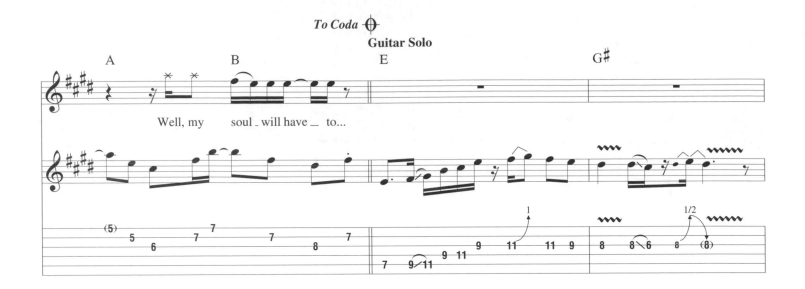

Well, my soul _ will have _ to...

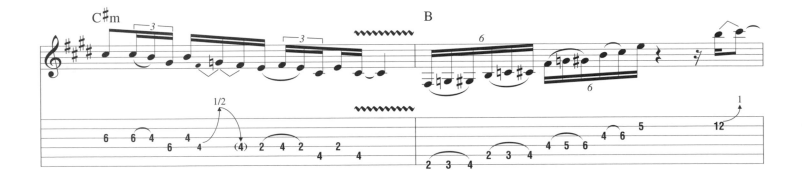

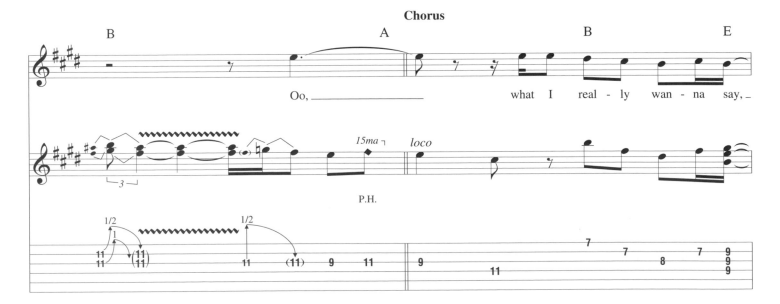

Oo, _____ what I real - ly wan - na say, _

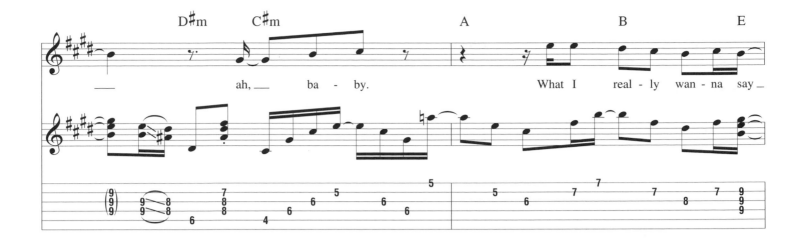

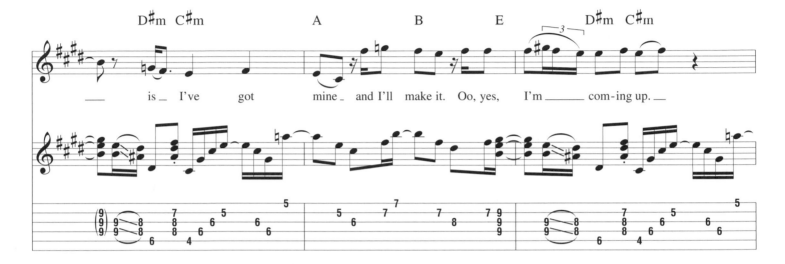

D.S. al Coda

𝄌 **Coda**

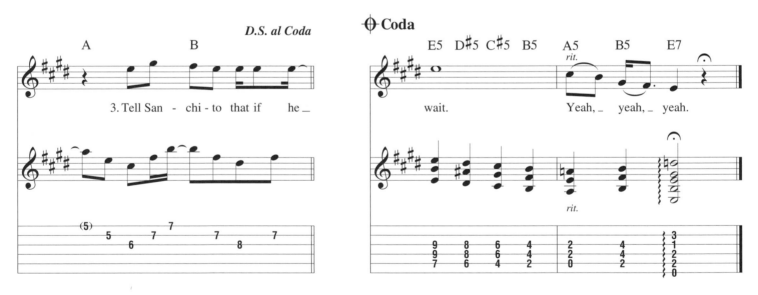

Additional Lyrics

3. Tell Sanchito that if he knows what is good for him
   He best go run and hide.
   Daddy's got a new .45
   And I won't think twice to stick that barrel
   Straight down Sancho's throat.
   Believe me when I say that I
   Got something for his punk ass.

Chorus What I really wanna know, my baby.
   Oo, what I really wanna say is there's just
   One way back and I'll make it.
   Yeah, my soul will have to wait. Yeah, yeah, yeah.

SAY IT AIN'T SO
Weezer

Video Lesson – 21 minutes, 23 seconds

Tune Down 1/2 Step: (low to high) E♭–A♭–D♭–G♭–B♭–E♭
Key of E

Guitar Tone:

- Guitar Tone 1:
  - ❯ clean tone
  - ❯ light reverb
  - ❯ bridge pickup
  - ❯ EQ: bass – 6, mid – 5, treble – 7

- Guitar Tone 2:
  - ❯ medium distortion
  - ❯ light reverb
  - ❯ bridge pickup
  - ❯ EQ: bass – 6, mid – 7, treble – 7

Chords:

Intro:

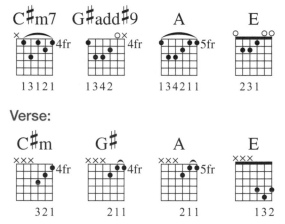

Verse:

Chorus:

C♯5/G♯   G♯5   A5   E5

Bridge:

B5   Bmaj7   G5

Techniques:

- Chordal Hammer-Ons: accuracy is key for the hammer-on employed in the main riff's C♯m7 chord. Make sure both fingers come down at the same time and land exactly on the correct strings. Form the interval in the air before landing the chord.

- Muted Strums: keep your fret hand lightly in contact with the strings, being careful not to accidentally fret any notes by pressing down too hard. Strum the muted strings, producing a "click" type sound.

- Rests: be mindful of the rests during the Verse. Mute the notes by damping with the pick hand, lifting off with the fret hand, or a combination of both.

Say It Ain't So

Words and Music by Rivers Cuomo

Tune down 1/2 step:
(low to high) E♭–A♭–D♭–G♭–B♭–E♭

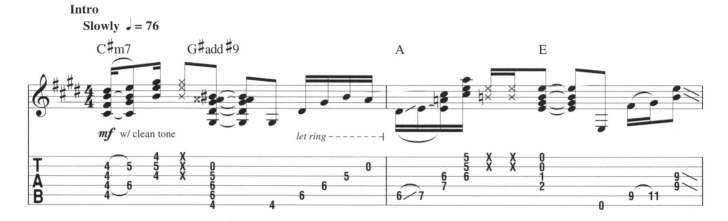

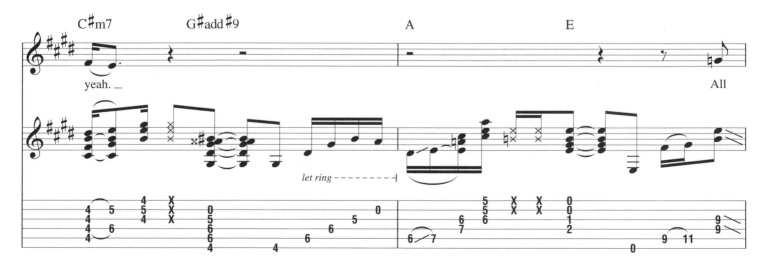

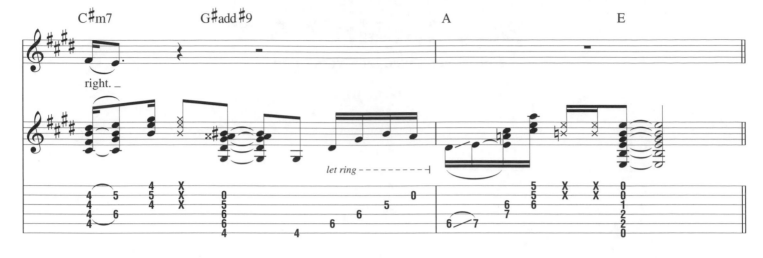

Verse

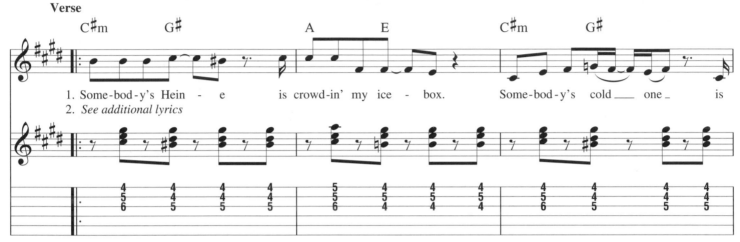

1. Some-bod-y's Hein — e   is crowd-in' my ice - box.   Some-bod-y's cold ___ one ___ is
2. *See additional lyrics*

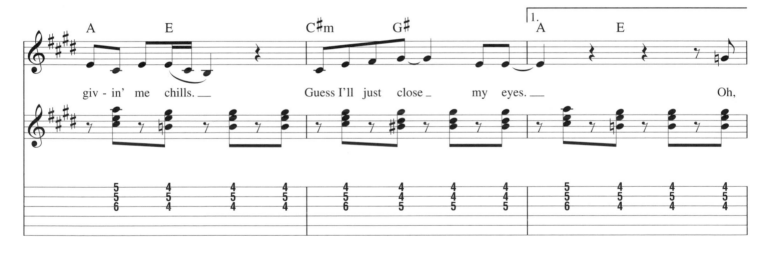

giv - in' me chills. ___   Guess I'll just close ___ my eyes. ___   Oh,

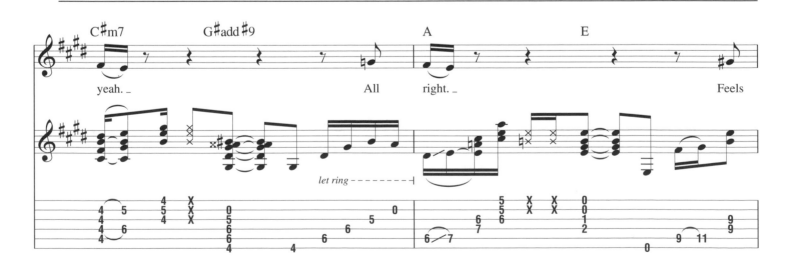

yeah. ___   All   right. ___   Feels

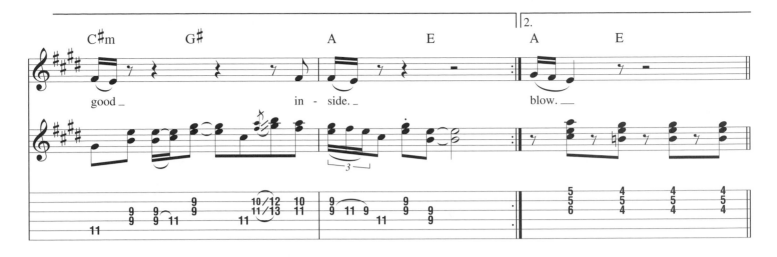

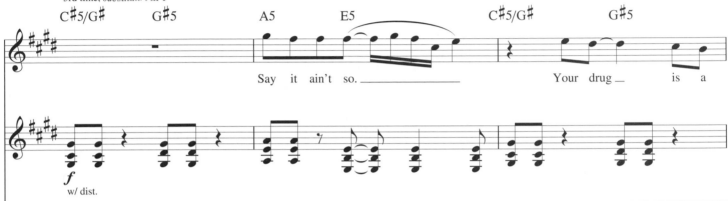

%‌ Chorus

3rd time, substitute Fill 1

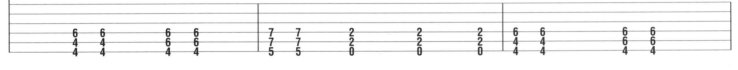

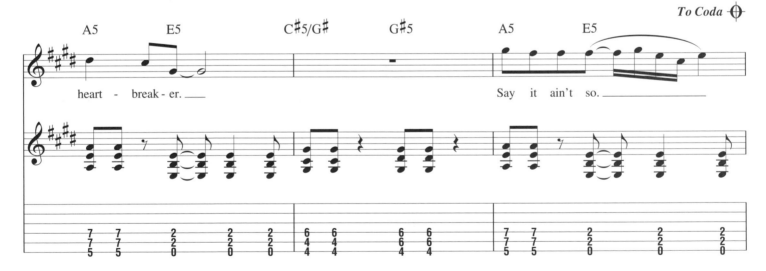

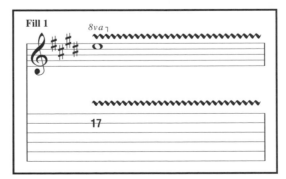

Interlude

My love __ is a life tak - er. __

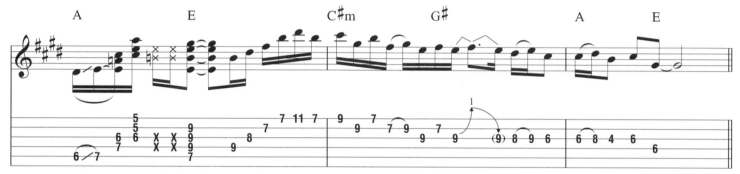

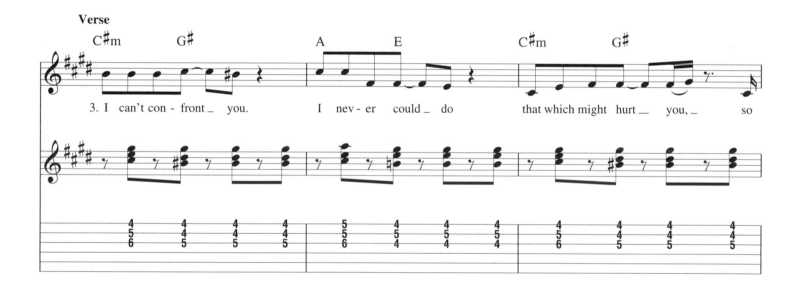

Verse

3. I can't con - front __ you. I nev - er could __ do that which might hurt __ you, __ so

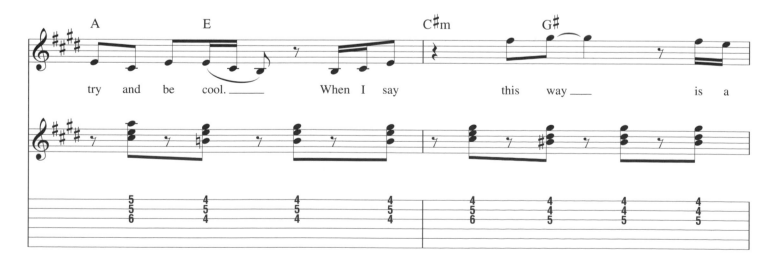

try and be cool. ____ When I say this way __ is a

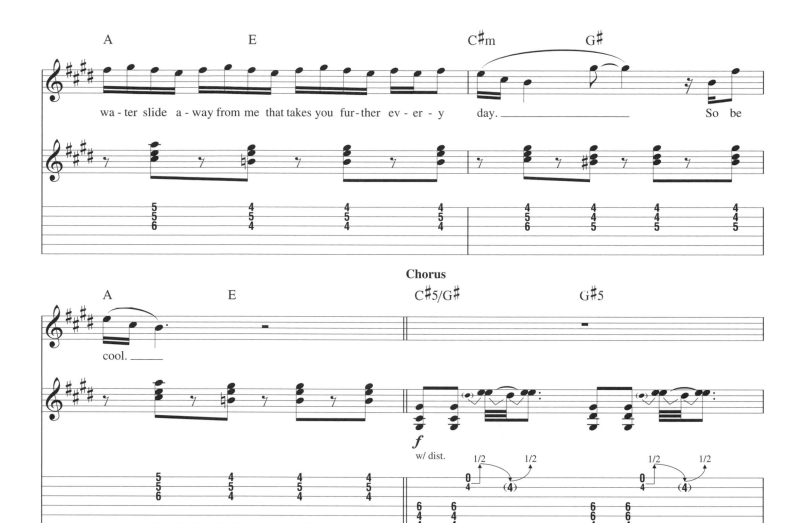

wa - ter slide a - way from me that takes you fur-ther ev - er - y day. _____ So be

Chorus

cool. _____

Say it ain't so. _____ Your drug __ is a heart - break-er. _____

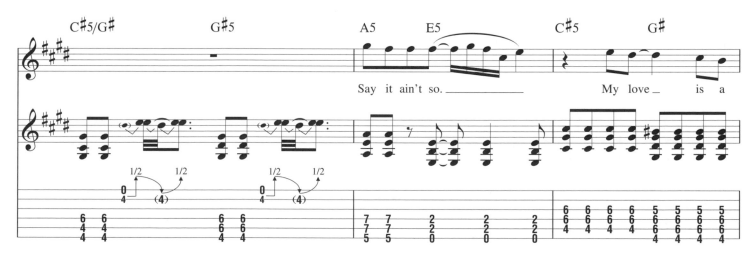

Say it ain't so. _____ My love __ is a

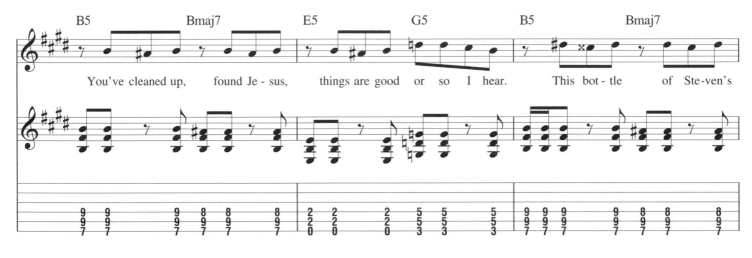

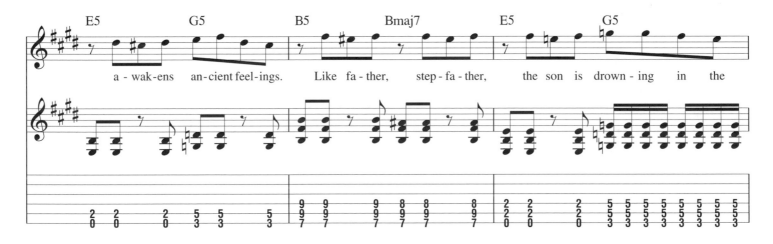

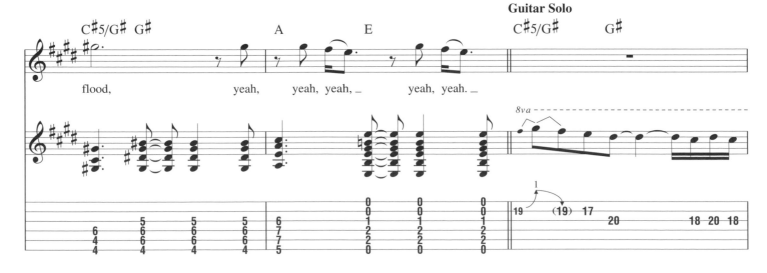

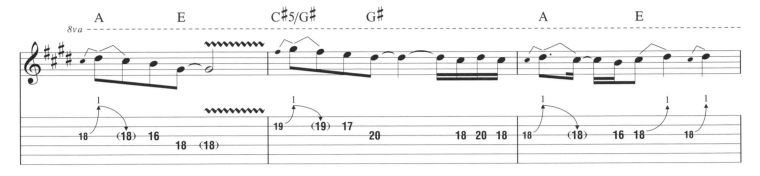

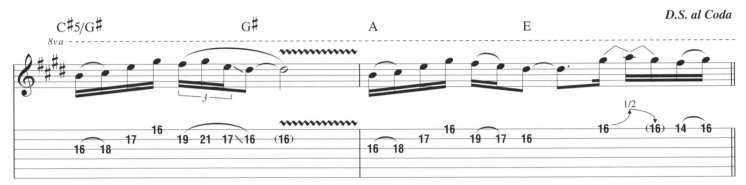

D.S. al Coda

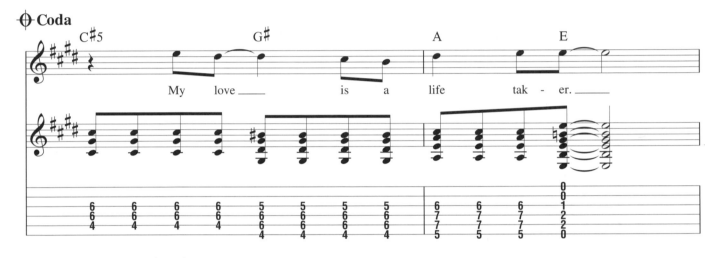

Coda

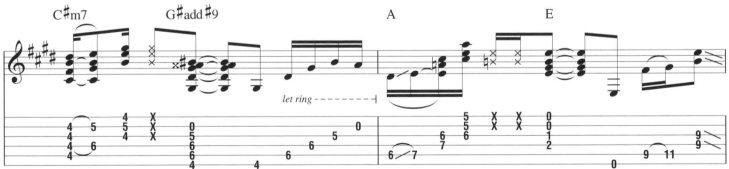

My love _____ is a life tak - er. _____

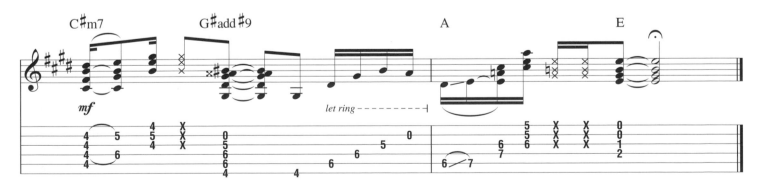

Additional Lyrics

2. Flip on the tele', wrestle with Jimmy.
   Something is a bubbling behind my back.
   The bottle is ready to blow.

21 GUNS
Green Day

Video Lesson – 14 minutes, 38 seconds

Standard Tuning: (low to high) E–A–D–G–B–E
Key of D minor

Guitar Tone:

- Guitar Tone 1:
    - ❱ electric guitar
    - ❱ clean tone
    - ❱ delay effect
    - ❱ EQ: bass – 5, mid – 5, treble – 7

- Guitar Tone 2:
    - ❱ electric guitar (or acoustic guitar)
    - ❱ clean tone
    - ❱ light reverb
    - ❱ EQ: bass – 5, mid – 5, treble – 7

- Guitar Tone 3 (Interlude):
    - ❱ electric guitar
    - ❱ medium distortion
    - ❱ light reverb
    - ❱ bridge pickup
    - ❱ EQ: bass – 5, mid – 5, treble – 7

Chords:

Verse:

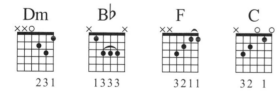

Chorus:

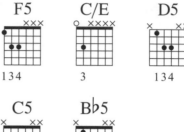

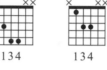

Bridge:

A5

Techniques:

- Volume Swells: during the Intro, start with your volume all the way off, pick the notes, and then bring the volume all the way up. Before playing the next notes, quickly return your volume to zero and start the process all over again.

- Open-Strum Transitions: use the open strummed notes during the Verse to allow for smoother chord changes. As you strum the open notes, prepare your fingers for the next chord.

- Rests: be mindful of the rests during the Chorus. Mute the notes by damping with your pick hand, lifting slightly off with your fret hand, or a combination of both.

21 Guns

Words and Music by David Bowie, John Phillips, Billie Joe and Green Day

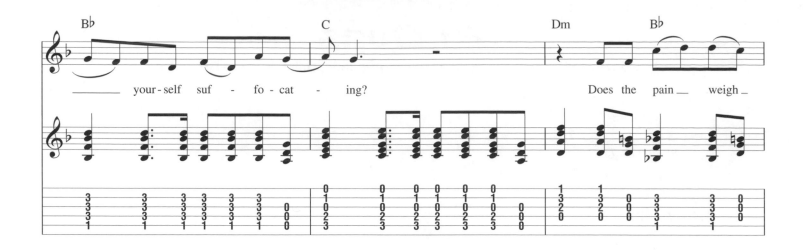

_____ your-self suf - fo - cat - ing? Does the pain _ weigh _

out _ the pride _____ and you look _ for a place _ to hide? _

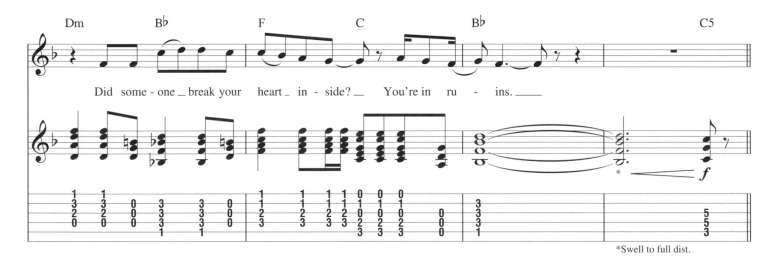

Did some - one _ break your heart _ in - side? _ You're in ru - ins. _____

*Swell to full dist.

𝄋 Chorus

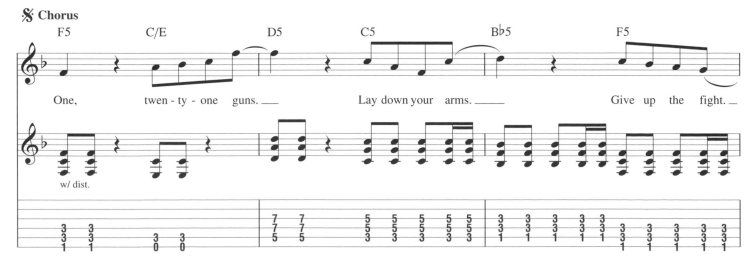

One, twen - ty - one guns. _ Lay down your arms. _____ Give up the fight. _

w/ dist.

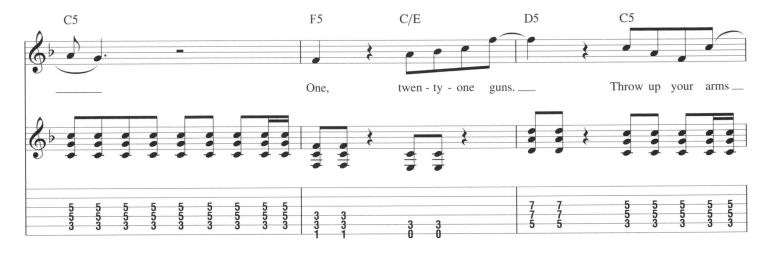

One, twen-ty-one guns. Throw up your arms

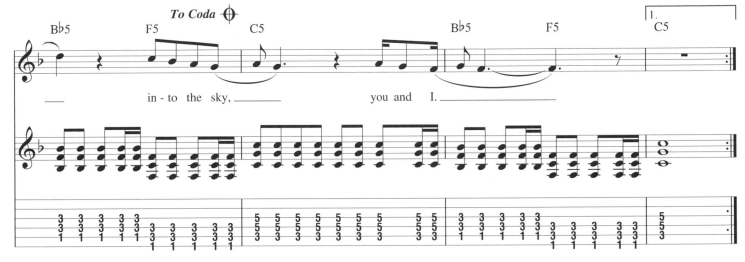

in-to the sky, you and I.

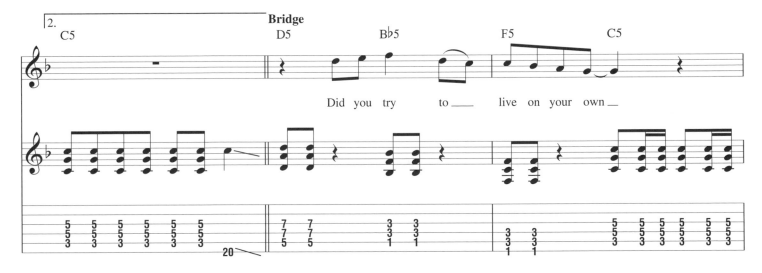

Did you try to live on your own

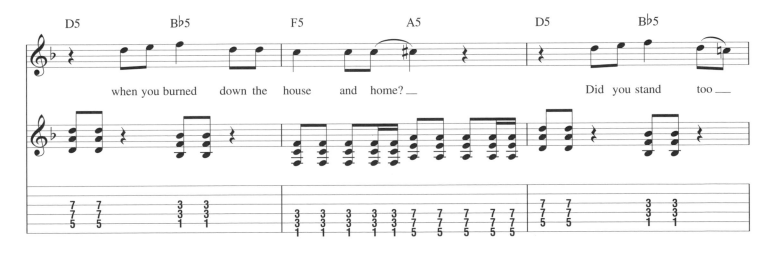

when you burned down the house and home? Did you stand too

close to the fire ___ like a li - ar look-ing for for-give - ness from a stone? ___

Interlude

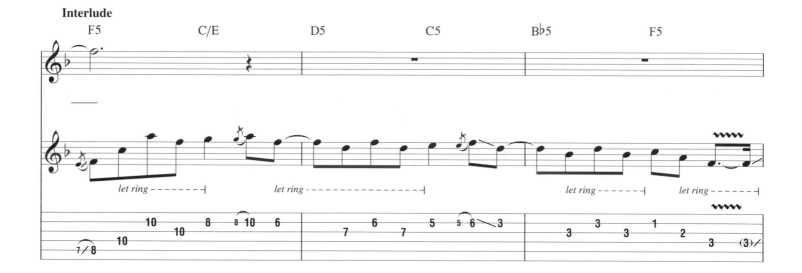

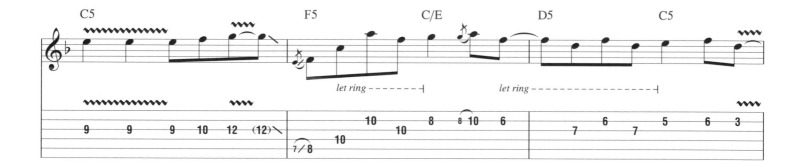

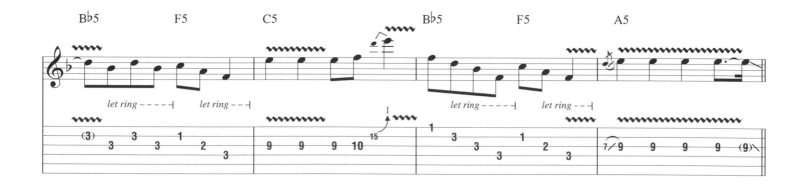

Interlude

Verse

3. When it's time to live and let die and you can't get an-

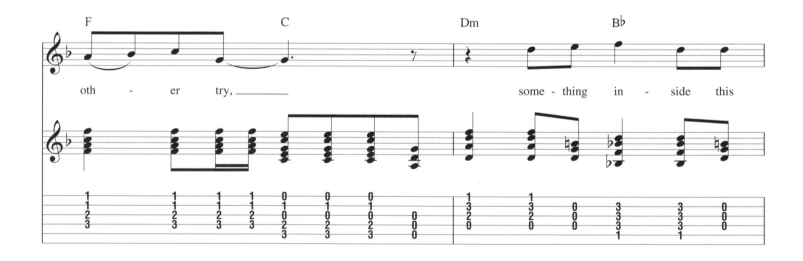

oth - er try, some - thing in - side this

D.S. al Coda

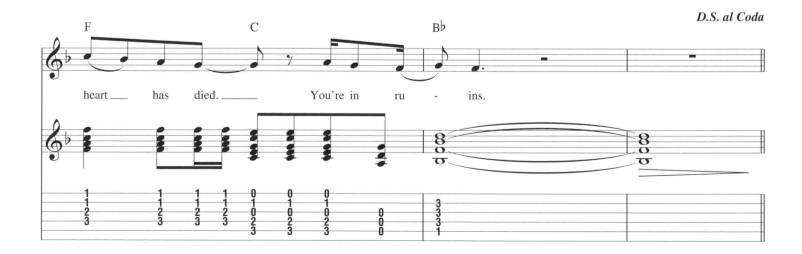

heart has died. You're in ru - ins.

Coda

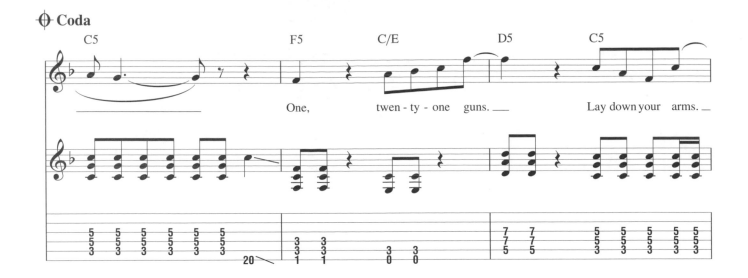

One, twen-ty-one guns. ___ Lay down your arms. ___

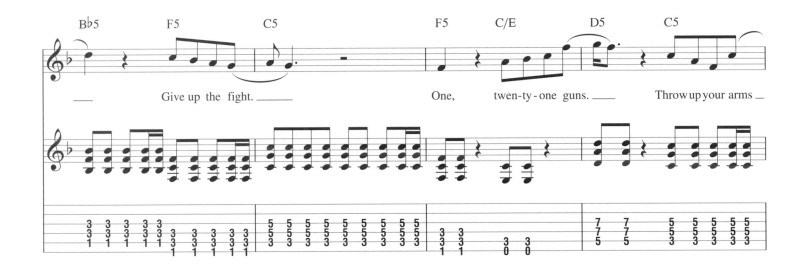

___ Give up the fight. _____ One, twen-ty-one guns. ___ Throw up your arms ___

___ in-to the sky, _____ you and I. _____

Additional Lyrics

2. When you're at the end of the road
   And you lost all sense of control.
   And your thoughts have taken their toll
   When your mind breaks the spirit of your soul.
   Your faith walks on broken glass
   And the hangover doesn't pass.
   Nothing's ever built to last.
   You're in ruins.

UNDER THE BRIDGE
Red Hot Chili Peppers

Video Lesson – 25 minutes, 38 seconds

Standard Tuning: (low to high) E–A–D–G–B–E
Key of D, E, and A

Guitar Tone:

- Guitar Tone 1:
  - ❯ clean tone
  - ❯ neck pickup
  - ❯ EQ: bass – 5, mid – 5, treble – 7

- Guitar Tone 2 (Bridge/Chorus/Outro):
  - ❯ light distortion
  - ❯ chorus effect
  - ❯ neck pickup
  - ❯ EQ: bass – 5, mid – 5, treble – 7

Chords:

Verse:

E	B	C#m
7fr	7fr	9fr
1 3 3 3	1 3 4 2 1	1 3 4 1 1

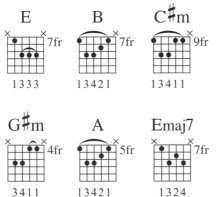

G#m	A	Emaj7
4fr	5fr	7fr
3 4 1 1	1 3 4 2 1	1 3 2 4

Pre-Chorus:

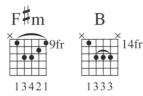

F#m	B
9fr	14fr
1 3 4 2 1	1 3 3 3

Bridge:

A	Am	G6	Fmaj7
5fr	5fr		
2 1	2 3	2 1	2 1

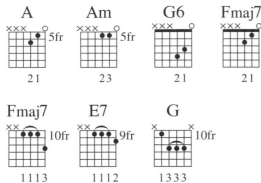

Fmaj7	E7	G
10fr	9fr	10fr
1 1 1 3	1 1 1 2	1 3 3 3

Chorus:

A	Am7	G6	Fmaj7
	5fr		
1 1 1	1 1 1	3 4 2 1	3 4 2 1

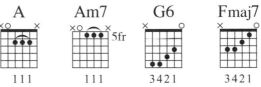

Arpeggios:

Intro:

D Arpeggio

F# Arpeggio

Techniques:

- Barre Chords: many types of barre chords are employed throughout this song. Keep your 1st finger straight and flat and make sure all fretted notes ring clearly. You might find it helpful to roll your 1st finger a bit to the outside (towards the thumb) to help it remain flat.

- Muted Strums: keep your fret hand lightly in contact with the strings, being careful not to accidentally fret any notes by pressing down too hard. Strum the muted strings, producing a "click" type sound.

- Open-String Chords: starting in the Bridge section, three-note open-string chords are used. Be sure to arch your fingers so you don't accidentally mute the open E string.

Under the Bridge

Words and Music by Anthony Kiedis, Flea, John Frusciante and Chad Smith

Intro

Moderately slow ♩ = 68

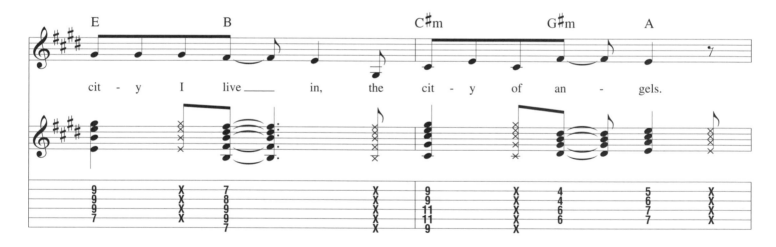

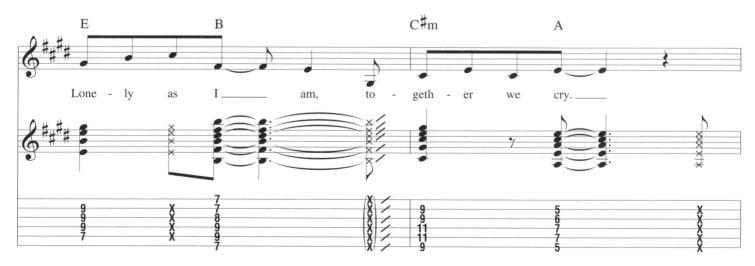

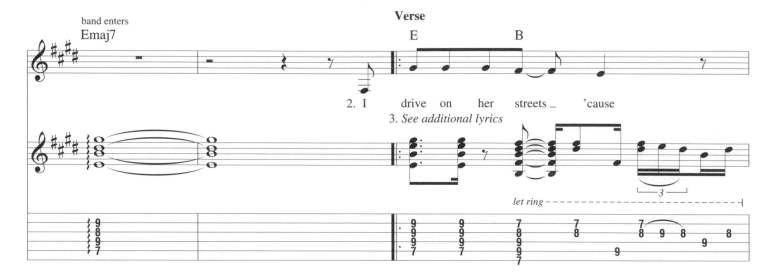

band enters

Emaj7

Verse

E   B

2. I drive on her streets __ 'cause
3. *See additional lyrics*

let ring

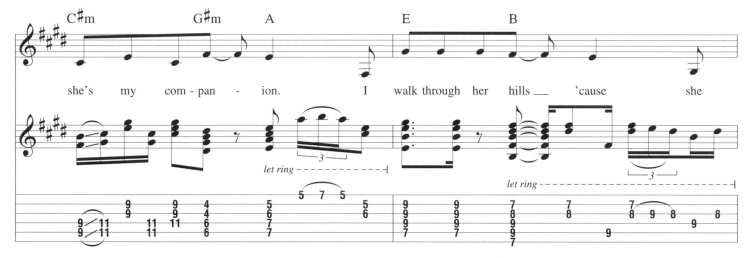

C#m   G#m   A   E   B

she's my com-pan-ion.   I walk through her hills __ 'cause she

let ring

let ring

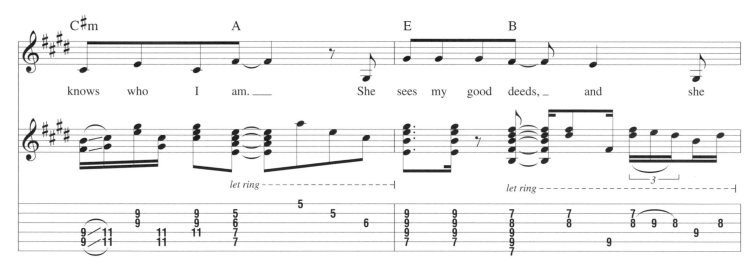

C#m   A   E   B

knows who I am. __   She sees my good deeds, __ and she

let ring

let ring

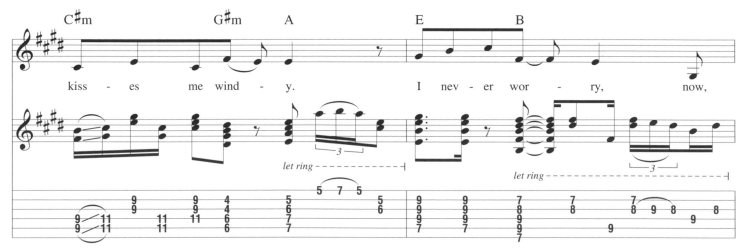

C#m   G#m   A   E   B

kiss-es me wind-y.   I nev-er wor-ry,   now,

let ring

let ring

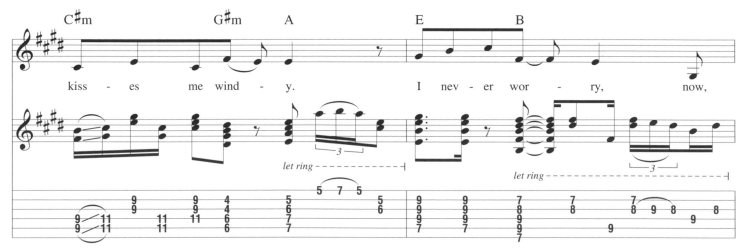

— 86 —

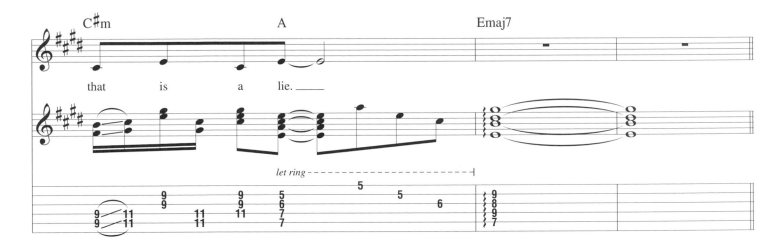

that is a lie. _____

Pre-Chorus

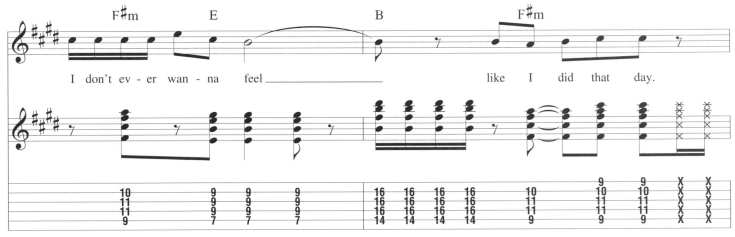

I don't ev - er wan - na feel _____ like I did that day.

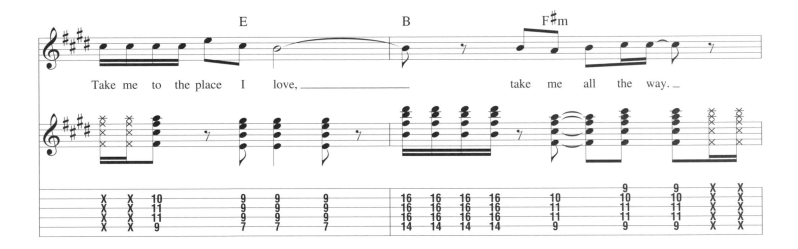

Take me to the place I love, _____ take me all the way. _

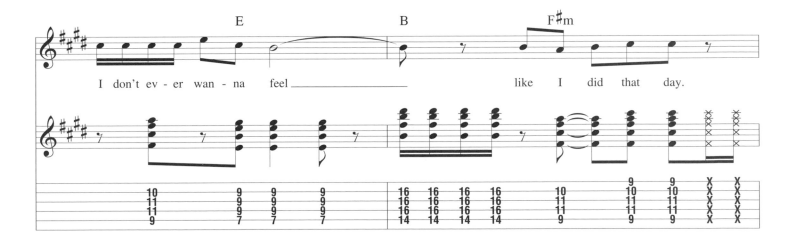

I don't ev - er wan - na feel _____ like I did that day.

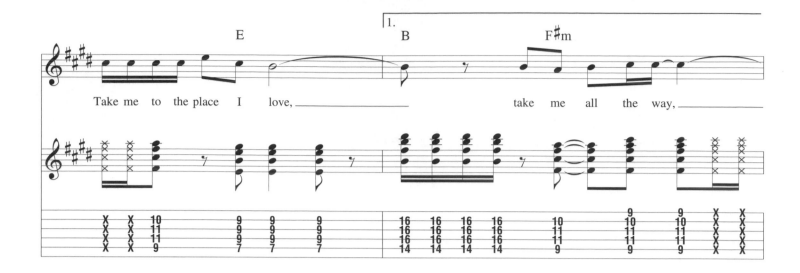

Take me to the place I love,_____ take me all the way,_____

_____ yeah._____ Yeah, yeah._____

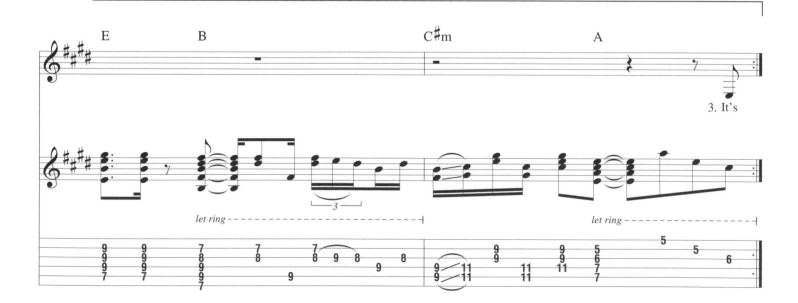

3. It's

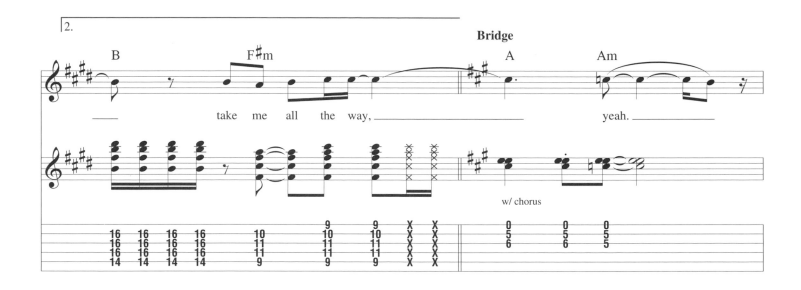

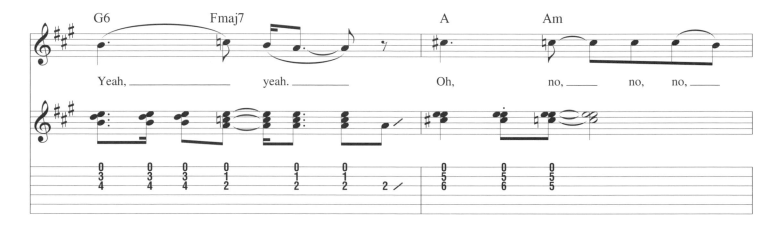

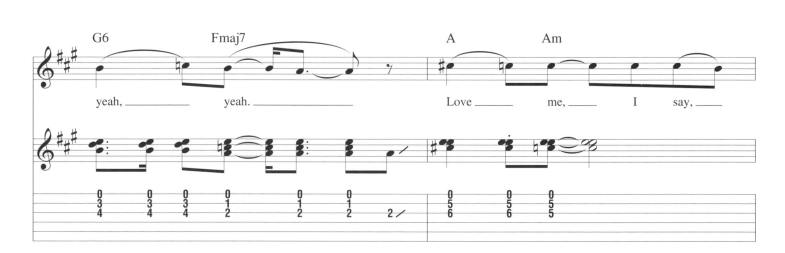

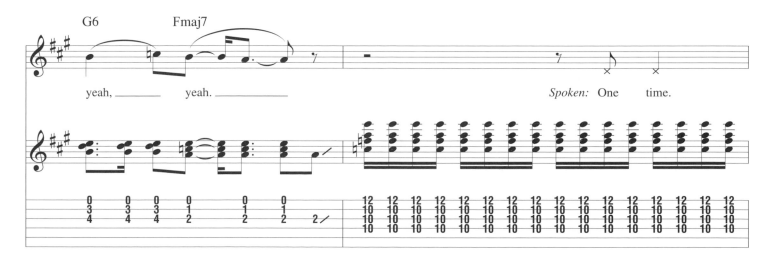

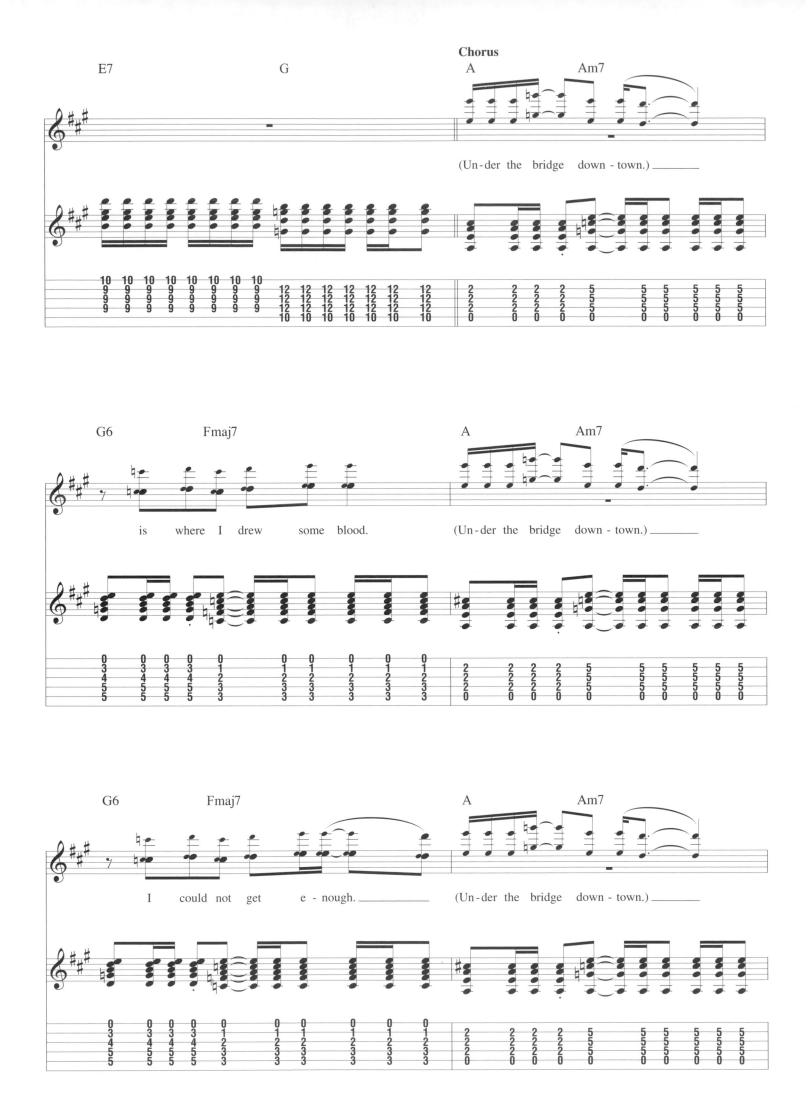

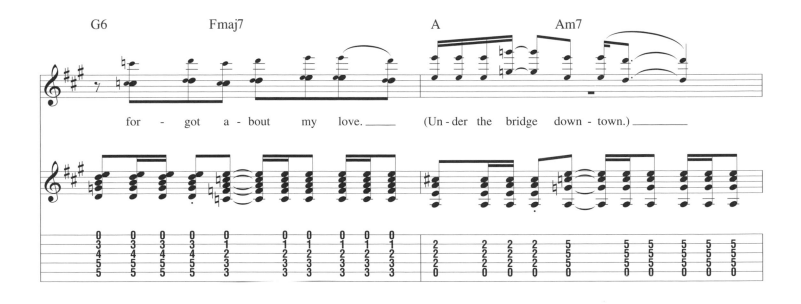

for - got a - bout my love. _____ (Un - der the bridge down - town.) _____

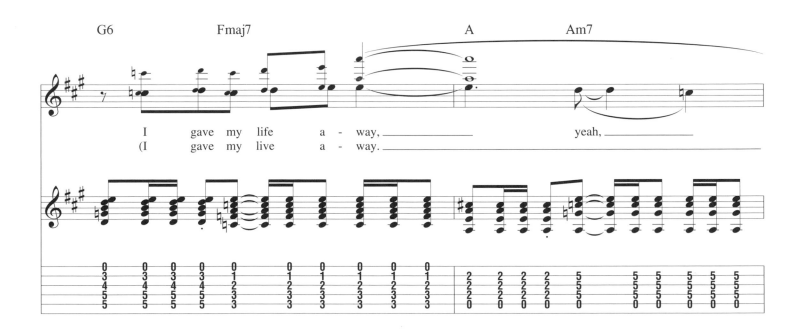

I gave my life a - way, _____ yeah, _____
(I gave my live a - way. _____

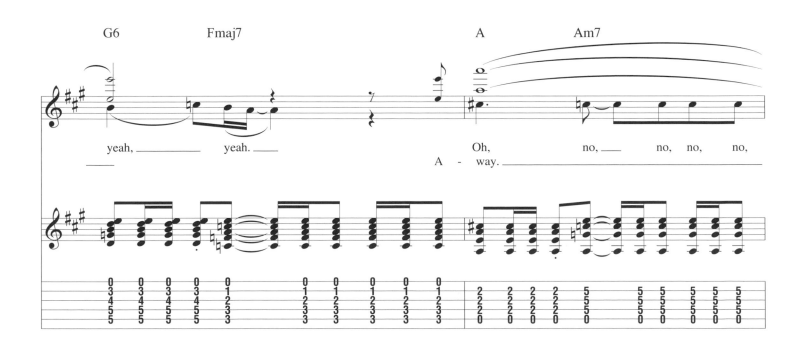

yeah, _____ yeah. _____ Oh, no, ___ no, no, no,
_____ A - way. _____

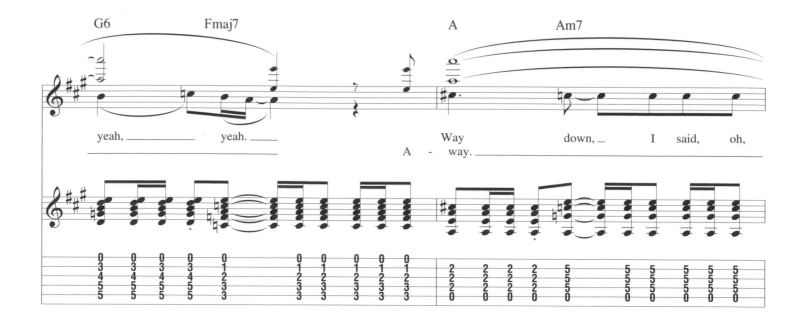

yeah, _____ yeah. _____

A - way. Way down, _ I said, oh,

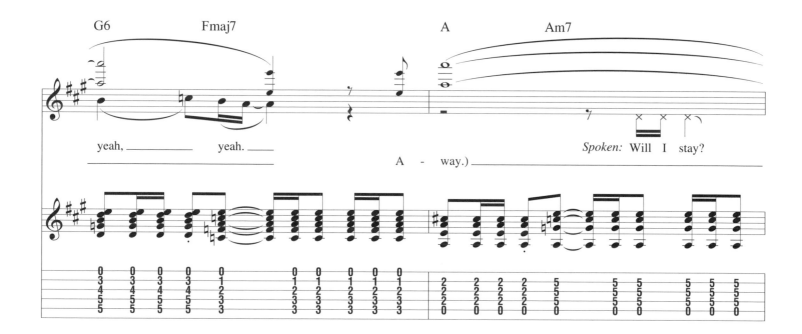

yeah, _____ yeah. _____

A - way.) _____ *Spoken:* Will I stay?

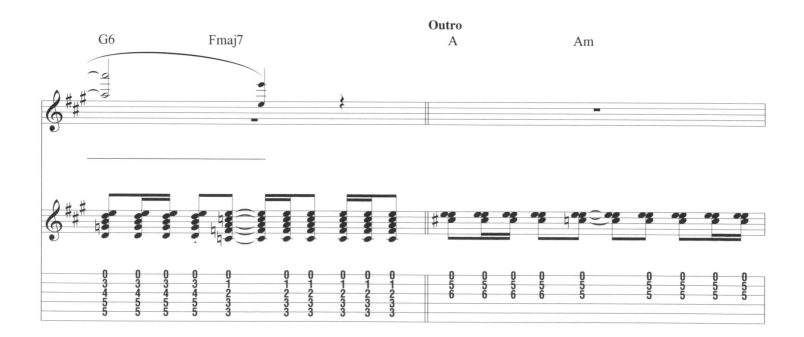

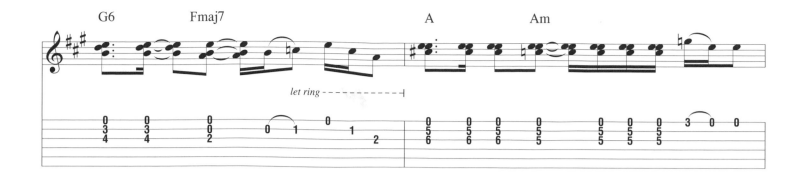

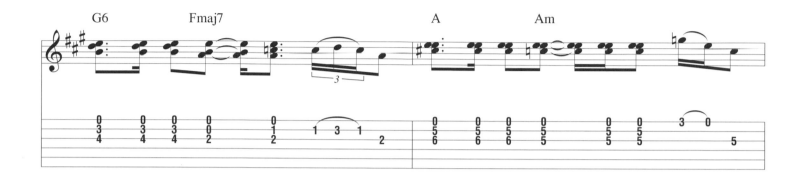

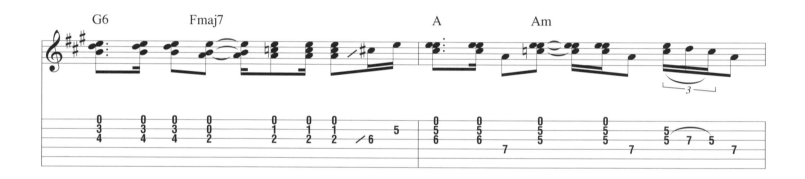

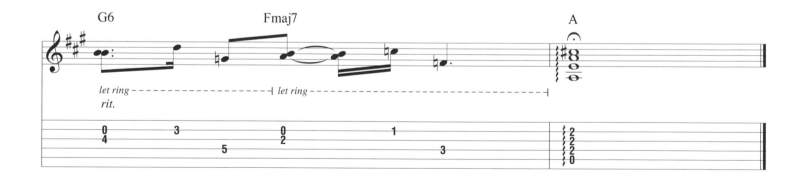

Additional Lyrics

3. It's hard to believe that there's nobody out there.
   It's hard to believe that I'm all alone.
   At least I have her love, the city, she loves me.
   Lonely as I am, together we cry.

GUITAR NOTATION LEGEND

THE MUSICAL STAFF shows pitches and rhythms and is divided by bar lines into measures. Pitches are named after the first seven letters of the alphabet.

TABLATURE graphically represents the guitar fingerboard. Each horizontal line represents a string, and each number represents a fret.

4th string, 2nd fret

1st & 2nd strings open, played together

open D chord

HALF-STEP BEND: Strike the note and bend up 1/2 step.

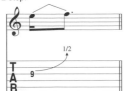

WHOLE-STEP BEND: Strike the note and bend up one step.

GRACE NOTE BEND: Strike the note and immediately bend up as indicated.

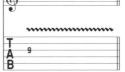

SLIGHT (MICROTONE) BEND: Strike the note and bend up 1/4 step.

BEND AND RELEASE: Strike the note and bend up as indicated, then release back to the original note. Only the first note is struck.

PRE-BEND: Bend the note as indicated, then strike it.

VIBRATO: The string is vibrated by rapidly bending and releasing the note with the fretting hand.

PALM MUTING: The note is partially muted by the pick hand lightly touching the string(s) just before the bridge.

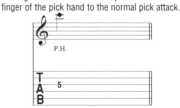

HAMMER-ON: Strike the first (lower) note with one finger, then sound the higher note (on the same string) with another finger by fretting it without picking.

PULL-OFF: Place both fingers on the notes to be sounded. Strike the first note and without picking, pull the finger off to sound the second (lower) note.

LEGATO SLIDE: Strike the first note and then slide the same fret-hand finger up or down to the second note. The second note is not struck.

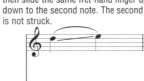

SHIFT SLIDE: Same as legato slide, except the second note is struck.

TRILL: Very rapidly alternate between the notes indicated by continuously hammering on and pulling off.

TAPPING: Hammer ("tap") the fret indicated with the pick-hand index or middle finger and pull off to the note fretted by the fret hand.

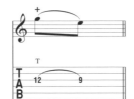

NATURAL HARMONIC: Strike the note while the fret-hand lightly touches the string directly over the fret indicated.

Harm.

PINCH HARMONIC: The note is fretted normally and a harmonic is produced by adding the edge of the thumb or the tip of the index finger of the pick hand to the normal pick attack.

P.H.

TREMOLO PICKING: The note is picked as rapidly and continuously as possible.

VIBRATO BAR DIVE AND RETURN: The pitch of the note or chord is dropped a specified number of steps (in rhythm), then returned to the original pitch.

w/ bar

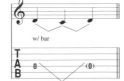

VIBRATO BAR SCOOP: Depress the bar just before striking the note, then quickly release the bar.

w/ bar

VIBRATO BAR DIP: Strike the note and then immediately drop a specified number of steps, then release back up to the original pitch.

w/ bar

Additional Musical Definitions

 *(accent)* · Accentuate note (play it louder).

(staccato) · Play the note short.

D.S. al Coda · Go back to the sign (𝄋), then play until the measure marked "***To Coda***," then skip to the section labelled "**Coda**."

D.C. al Fine · Go back to the beginning of the song and play until the measure marked "***Fine***" (end).

Fill · Label used to identify a brief melodic figure which is to be inserted into the arrangement.

N.C. · Harmony is implied.

· Repeat measures between signs.

· When a repeated section has different endings, play the first ending only the first time and the second ending only the second time.